Case Studies in Sport Marketing

Brenda G. Pitts, Ed.D.
Editor
Florida State University

Fitness Information Technology, Inc.
Morgantown, WV

Library of Congress Card Catalog Number: 98-71809

ISBN 1-885693-13-3

Copyeditor: Sandra R. Woods
Cover Design: Pegasus
Production Editor: Craig Hines
Printed by: BookCrafters

Printed in the United States of America
10 9 8 7 6 5 4 3 2 1

Fitness Information Technology, Inc.
P.O. Box 4425, University Avenue
Morgantown, WV 26504–4425
(800) 477–4348
(304) 599–3482 (Phone/Fax)
E-mail: fit@fitinfotech.com
www.fitinfotech.com

Sport Management Library

The Sport Management Library is an integrative textbook series targeted toward undergraduate students. The titles included in the library are reflective of the content areas prescribed by the NASPE/NASSM curriculum standards for the undergraduate sport management programs.

Titles in the Sport Management Library
Ethics in Sport Management
Financing Sport
Fundamentals of Sport Marketing
Legal Aspects of Sport Entrepreneurship
Sport Facility Planning and Management
Sport Governance in the Global Community
Sport Management Field Experiences

Forthcoming Titles
Communication in Sport Organizations
Economics of Sport

ABOUT THE EDITOR

Dr. Brenda G. Pitts is a graduate of the University of Alabama. She is currently with the faculty of sport management at the Florida State University. She teaches undergraduate and graduate courses including Sport Marketing, Sport Administration, and Research in Sport Administration. She has taught Sport Marketing around the world including Hong Kong, Singapore and Malaysia. Her research has been published in numerous journals including the *Journal of Sport Management, Sport Marketing Quarterly, Journal of Sport and Social Issues, Leisure Information Quarterly, Journal of Legal Aspects of Sport,* and *Women in Sport and Physical Activity Journal*. She is the co-author for the *Fundamentals of Sport Marketing* textbook, co-authored a chapter title "Strategic Sport Marketing: Case Analysis," is currently working on two books on the lesbian and gay sport market, and has given numerous scholarly presentations at national and international conferences. Her research foci include sport marketing, sport management curriculum, and sport and sport management in the lesbian and gay community.

Dr. Pitts' professional service contributions have included serving the North American Society for Sport Management as an officer for five years and in other various capacities, serving as Co-Chair of the NASPE-NASSM Task Force on Sport Management Curriculum Standards for seven years, as a member of the Sport Management Program Review Council for three years, and organized the first research conference on lesbian and gay people and sport held in conjunction with the Gay Games IV in New York in 1994.

A former collegiate and professional basketball player, Dr. Pitts is a member of the Huntsville-Madison County Sports Hall of Fame and continues to pursue her lifelong interests in sport and sport management through participation and occasionally managing sports such as soccer, golf, boating, softball, camping, and volleyball.

ABOUT THE CONTRIBUTING AUTHORS

F. Wayne Blann earned a doctor of education degree from Boston University, and currently serves as professor of sport sciences and coordinator of sport management at Ithaca College. Dr. Blann pioneered research on American collegiate and professional athletes' career transitions and Australian elite amateur and professional athletes' and coaches' career transitions. He has served as consultant to the National Basketball Association, National Football League, National Hockey League Players' Association, and Major League Baseball Players' Association regarding players' development programs. Beginning in 1996, the "Professional Athletes Career Transition Program" (PACTP) developed by Dr. Blann has served as the model for athlete career education programs being implemented by the Australian Institute of Sport and at each of the Australian state institutes of sport. He has given numerous presentations at national and international conferences and has published articles in sport management, applied sport psychology, sport sociology, and applied research in coaching and athletics journals and newsletters. As a former collegiate athlete, coach, and athletic director, Dr. Blann is an honorary member of the Jouhnson State College, Vermont, Sports Hall of Fame.

Jacquelyn Cuneen, Ed. D., is a Sport Management Field Experience Coordinator at Bowling Green State University. Her primary research foci are professional preparation in sport management and sport and event marketing. She has authored or co-authored articles appearing in the *Journal of Sport Management, Sex Roles, Sport Marketing Quarterly, Journal of Physical Education, Recreation, and Dance, Schole*, and others. Prior to coming to BGSU, she was Account Executive, Continuity

Director and Director of Women's Programming for two ABC Radio affiliates in New York's Capitol District, and Southern Tier. She has been a member of the NASSM Executive Council, the Graduate Sport Management Program Advisory Board for West Virginia University, and various other professional committees. Dr. Cuneen was a visiting scholar for the North Carolina Center for Independent Higher Education in 1992.

Dianna P. Gray, Ph.D., Associate Professor, University of Northern Colorado, Greeley, Colorado

Dianna Gray received her B.S. from James Madison University and her M.S. and Ph.D. from The Ohio State University. Currently, she is a faculty member in the sport administration graduate program at the University of Northern Colorado. She is also a consultant and author in the areas of sport marketing and public relations. She has presented at NASSM, EASM, AAHPERD, and at various international conferences. Dr. Gray currently serves on the advisory board of the Women's Sport Foundation and the Sport and Entertainment Academy, Indiana University.

Richard L. Irwin, Ed.D., Associate Professor University of Memphis.

Dr. Irwin joined the University of Memphis Department of Human Movement Sciences & Education faculty in 1994 following four years as an assistant professor at Kent State Univeristy. In addition to serving as coordinator for the Recreation, Leisure & Sport Studies Unit (comprising of the undergraduate sport and leisure studies and graduate sport and leisure commerce degree programs), Dr. Irwin is also the director of the Bureau of Sport and Leisure Commerce at the University of Memphis. As director of the University of Memphis Bureau of Sport & Leisure Commerce, Dr. Irwin has been responsible for generating over a quarter of a million dollars in external funding. Funded research and service projects have been conducted on behalf of local and national sponsors such as the National Collegiate Athletic Association, Women's Basketball Association, Memphis Convention and Visitors Bureau, FedEx St. Jude Golf Classic, and Memphis AAA Baseball. Additionally, Dr. Irwin is co-principal of Audience Analysts, a sport market research company, which has consulted with several professional sport franchises including the Orlando Magic, Cleveland Cavaliers, Philadelphia 76ers, and Indiana Pacers. His scholarly research track has typically focused on sport and leisure marketing management as reflected by published works on the topics of sport sponsorship, and licensing, as well as consumer behavior and servicing. Dr. Irwin also serves as a member of the North American Society of Sport Management Executive Council, the *Sport Marketing Quarterly* Editorial Board, and the AXA/Equitable Liberty Bowl Board of Directors.

Dr. David K. Stotlar has a Doctor of Education degree from the University of Utah and teaches on the faculty at the University of Northern Colorado in the areas of sport management and sport law. He has had over 40 articles published in professional journals and has written several textbooks and book chapters in sport, fitness, and physical education. He has made numerous presentations at international and national professional conferences. On several occasions, he has served as a consultant to fitness and sport professionals and, in the area of sport law, to attorneys and international sport administrations. He was selected by the USOC as a delegate to the International Olympic Academy in Greece and the World University Games Forum in Italy. He has conducted international seminars in sport management for the Hong Kong Olympic Committee, the National Sport Council of Malaysia, Mauritius National Sports Council, the National Sports Council of Zimbabwe, the Singapore Sports Council, the Chinese Taipei University Sport Federation, the Bahrain Sport Institute, the government of Saudi Arabia, the South African National Sports Congress, and the Association of Sport Sciences in South Africa. Dr. Stotlar's contribution to the profession includes having served as the chair of the Council on Facilities and Equipment of the American Alliance for Health, Physical Education, Recreation and Dance as a board member and later as president of the North American Society for Sport Management.

TABLE OF CONTENTS

FOREWORD

The use of case studies in sport management education is a growing trend. This is exemplified by this publication specifically relating to a series of sport marketing case studies. Case study teaching is a popular method of teaching within business schools throughout the world. This is a significant point as I note the alignment of sport management education towards business schools and associated management and business teaching methodologies. As the author points out in this text, case study teaching offers the opportunity to simulate the real world in the classroom. Based on the information presented in the case, students are able to exercise and apply their problem-solving skills in the same way managers do within businesses and sporting organisations.

This text highlights the emphasis on preparing students for managerial decision making within an increasingly business oriented sports sector. It is difficult to provide students with living, breathing organisations to study for obvious reasons. Case study analysis simulates, as best we can as educators, the business and managerial framework within which decisions are formulated. There are no right or wrong answers to arise from case study analysis, only those that appear to be better argued and logically presented given the circumstances confronting the manager. The text does an excellent job in extolling the benefits of case study analysis. The value of the cases presented in this text are further reinforced via the link to the text *Fundamentals of Sport Marketing* by Pitts and Stotlar (1996) which provides the theoretical bases upon which the case studies can be evaluated.

Another feature of the text is the industry segmentation model used to group the case studies, further demonstrating our increasing understanding of the diversity and complexity of organisations comprising the sport industry. There are five cases in each section covering a variety of sports and related organisations, perspectives and dilemmas confronting the sport marketing manager. In the sports performance industry segment the nuances of marketing events are developed, as is the importance of gender equity in participatory programs, the use of situation analysis and its importance in determining marketing strategies and finally the challenges of filling stadia for sporting events. The sport production industry segment provides a more traditional application of marketing theory. This section reinforces the challenges of marketing goods as opposed to services as outlined in the first five case studies. Students should note the subtle differences in marketing theory as it applies to services and marketing sport, in contrast to marketing goods such as football helmets, turf and associated equipment and the important sporting goods industry.

The final segment is the sport promotion industry which allows students the opportunity to examine how sport acts as a conduit for organisations to promote and subsequently sell product. Sponsorship is central to this sector. As an Australian fortunate enough to be in the USA when Australia wrested the America's Cup from the U.S. in 1983 I enjoyed reading this case study. Prior to 1983 the America's Cup had never been won by any other nation other than the USA. The event is steeped in tradition, as was the New York Yacht Club, responsible for the conduct of the event until 1983. This case study is interesting because it demonstrates how the America's Cup became more attractive to sponsors as the conservative traditions of the New York Yacht Club dissipated. It also highlights the challenges of sponsoring sport when the outcome can never be guaranteed.

This textbook is a welcome addition to the range of sport management related resources designed to improve the level of instruction in the classroom. As indicated it covers an interesting array of case studies specific to sport marketing. The organisation of the case studies and the supporting theory available through *Fundamentals of Sport Marketing* provide a comprehensive package for the instructor and student. Students are also provided with extensive advice on how to analyse and use case studies in the classroom. I urge students to carefully read this section before embarking on the exploration of solutions. Students should also use the knowledge and guidance provided by their instructors to assist their analysis and learn to appreciate the evolution of solutions to emerge from working with their fellow students in the analysis of the case studies. Even in a changing world of corporate organisation, information sharing and discussion form the basis of solid managerial decision making. I wish students and instructors well in their use of this valuable resource and recommend its use to all those studying sport marketing. I also congratulate Dr. Brenda Pitts as editor, responsible for bringing together five contributing authors whose dedication to providing the very best in sport management educational resources will be appreciated by many students.

David Shilbury, Ph.D.
Coordinator Sport Management Program
Deakin University
221 Burwood Highway
Burwood 3125
Melbourne, Australia
shilbury@deakin.edu.au

PREFACE

The sport business industry is a challenging and exciting business. It is a multibillion-dollar industry and ranks as the 11th largest industry in the United States. In this large and complex industry, the need for specially educated sport management professionals is at an all-time high. Based on the popularity of sport and its pervasive place in our daily lives, the industry will continue to grow and develop. The need for sport management professionals will increase in relation to this growth. Moreover, as the sport industry continues to grow in variety, scope, and specialty, there will be an increased need for sport management professionals with specializations. The need for specialization exists today.

There are a variety of careers one may pursue. This is the topic of an entire book edited by Parks, Zanger and Quarterman (1998). In the future, sport management degree programs will offer specializations such as sport marketing, management in the fitness industry, sport information, athletic administration, sporting goods industry, resort and country club management, sport law and others. Although a few colleges and universities already offer some of these specializations, more will be added as programs develop.

In the past, sport professionals enjoyed the popularity and growth of sport without having to acquire a specialized education. A person with at least a degree in physical education or recreation seemed to be best prepared. However, those were the days of simplicity. The highly competitive nature of the sport business industry today requires that a person seeking a career in the sport industry acquire a complex mix of talents and a wealth of specialized knowledge and skills. From this need grows our new field of study, sport management. This involves degree programs designed specifically to prepare individuals for the sport business industry. The knowledge base of sport management includes financial management in sport, sport marketing, sport sociology, economics of the sport business, personnel management in sport, computer applications in sport, legal aspects of sport, and other important subject areas.

This book is for individuals interested in a career in sport management and in particular in sport marketing. Sport marketing is an important specialization. Marketing is the one aspect of a business that makes it or breaks it. Sport marketing personnel must make educated and strategic decisions in today's rapidly changing local, national, and world markets. One of the most successful methods for teaching students to critically analyze sport business situations and make educated decisions is the case study method.

This book is a sport marketing case study book. The primary purpose for this book is for students to apply what they have learned about sport marketing principles and concepts to simulated sport business situations. Further, it was written to help the student obtain a high level of competency in critical analysis, problem identification, decision making, and solution development.

In addition, this book was written for the sport marketing instructor. Sport management and sport marketing instructors are always searching for course material and sport business case studies and for ways to make their courses a more meaningful learning experience for their students. The objective is to make the course material more relevant by using real situations. This book provides a key resource and will help the instructor by serving as a model for new courses and as a tool for existing courses.

Features

The book is divided into two parts. Part One contains two chapters. They are written as overview chapters and should not be considered conclusive. They provide a starting point. There are many case analysis models in general marketing literature that could be used in sport marketing case analysis. The reader is encouraged to try more than one model in order to find one that works best for her or him.

Part Two contains the cases in three sections. The sections reflect the three industry segments developed in sport marketing research in an industry segmentation model by Pitts, Fielding, and Miller (1994) (see appendix). This model offers a unique way of looking at the sport industry by categorizing products according to product function. A sport marketer needs to understand the functions, utility and benefits that a consumer is looking for in a product. For example, Erin wants a better batting average, more hits and home runs, and better hitting control in softball. Erin must have a product that will provide those functions and benefits. Therefore, the marketer must understand that the company is providing a product whose functions will be to increase batting average, hits, home runs, and improve hitting control.

The cases in this book were selected based on reality, various marketing problems in different marketing areas, and a variety of sport industry settings. Some contain issues that challenge sport management professionals. Some issues today that affect the sport business industry include environmental concern, human rights, economics, politics, the world as market place, global humanity, and others. The intent is to place the student in situations that depict the world today and in the future.

The cases vary in length and complexity. This does not mean that a short case is a simple case. A case of any length may challenge the student's knowledge of basic sport marketing principles and the student's creative and analytical skills.

None of the cases contain all the facts relevant to or existing in the specific situation presented. This challenges the student to learn to detect "black holes" in information and then to make educated assumptions.

How to Use This Book

This book may be used as a single text for a class or may be used in conjunction with other textbooks or course materials. In many situations, the instructor has already prepared case study materials and has no textbook. I believe the instructor will find this book useful as a text and as a secondary resource.

In addition, although this book is intended for use in undergraduate sport marketing and sport marketing case study courses, it may be used in a variety of classes and may even be useful to practitioners. The reader is encouraged to review its content for potential use in a variety of situations.

Finally, this book was written to be a companion book to *Fundamentals of Sport Marketing* (Pitts and Stotlar, 1996). All cases are based on those basic fundamentals of sport marketing as found in Pitts and Stotlar. The book could also be used for graduate seminar courses on sport marketing. There are 15 cases, which would allow the use of one case per week in a typical 15-week semester.

References

Parks, J. B., Zanger, B., & Quarterman, J. (1998). *Contemporary sport management.* Champaign, IL: Human Kinetics.

Pitts, B. G., Fielding, L. W., & Miller, L. K. (1994). Industry segmentation theory and the sport industry: Developing a sport industry segment model. *Sport Marketing Quarterly, 3* (1), 15–24.

Pitts, B. G., & Stotlar, D. K. (1996). *Fundamentals of sport marketing.* Morgantown, WV: Fitness Information Technology.

ACKNOWLEDGMENTS

There are many people to be recognized for their help and contributions in a variety of capacities to bring this book to reality. Each person's contributions are appreciated, and I would like to recognize them. First, I want to thank the contributing authors. They are some of the best faculty in sport marketing, all of whom are well known in sport management in the United States, some of whom are recognized around the world for their expertise. They have worked long and hard to bring to the field the first case study book in sport marketing. I think the reader will agree that the cases are extraordinary.

I want to thank Janet Parks and the editorial board of the Sport Management Library (SML). The SML is a significant contribution to sport management. Many of the books are the first of their kind and will serve as the foundation upon which future books are written. Dr. Parks has been the guiding force for the SML and deserves our highest recognition for her vision, leadership, and work.

Charlie Song (San Jose State University) and Denny Ruth Kelley (University of Tennessee) provided exceptional critical reviews of earlier drafts of this manuscript. Their analysis and vision for changes toward creating a much better and more user-friendly book were significant. The contributing authors join me in thanking them.

Earlier versions and drafts of this manuscript were tested in one of my courses and by Denny Ruth Kelley in one of her courses. Our students' evaluations and feedback were very helpful. I appreciate their help and appreciate Dr. Kelley's willingness to test the cases. Thank you.

Karen Groves, a computer graphics design specialist, turned the tables and graphs into neat and professional works of art. Thank you, Karen.

Finally, I want to thank the real companies who gave us permission to write about their businesses and who have released their information for this book. We hope this partnership between sport management education and the sport industry will continue and we will work with other companies in future editions of this book.

PART I

. . . .

An Introduction to the Case Study Method

CHAPTER 1

An Introduction to the Case Study Method

The Sport Industry, Sport Management, and Sport Marketing

The sport industry is "the market in which the products offered to its buyers are sport, fitness, recreation, or leisure-related and may be activities, goods, services, people, places, or ideas" (Pitts & Stotlar, 1996, p. 3). The sport industry is enormous and varied, consisting of a great variety of companies, organizations, and products. Students who want a career in the sport industry are majoring in sport management, the young and emerging field of study that prepares one to enter the sport industry. Sport management is "all people, activities, businesses, and organizations involved in producing, facilitating, promoting, or organizing sports, fitness, and recreation products" (Pitts & Stotlar, 1996, p. 2). The sport industry consists of much more than people who are directly involved with managing sports. For example, the industry includes those companies that manufacture equipment or promotional merchandise; those businesses that produce uniforms and other apparel or shoes; services such as racket stringing, golf club cleaning, or laundry; professional services such as legal advice, promotional advice, or advertising; and those companies that design, build, or manage sports facilities.

Sport marketing is one aspect of sport management and is "the process of designing and implementing activities for the production, pricing, promotion, and distribution of a sport product to satisfy the needs or desires of consumers and to achieve the company's objectives" (Pitts & Stotlar, 1996, p. 80). It is a major management function for any sport business and requires continual strategic planning. A student in sport management must acquire sport management, including sport marketing, skills and knowledge. Using case studies is a method for gaining some of the knowledge and skill needed. It allows the student a real look at situations that exist in the sport business industry. The cases involve a variety of sport business settings and include a variety of marketing problems that the student may face.

Introduction to Case Study

In sport management curricula, students are expected to learn a base of knowledge, master analytical and conceptual thinking, become prepared to successfully meet the challenges of the real world and the sport business industry, and develop the ability to deal with the daily issues and problems to be confronted in their profession and at their workplace. Most curricula in sport management provide the field experience as a way for students to apply what they are learning, be exposed to and learn about a real sport business, and gain practical experience. Additionally, many instructors in sport management are increasingly using case study. Using cases, students practice the fundamentals of sport management in the classroom and learn to analyze a situation and recommend appropriate action if needed. One of the primary differences between field experience and case analysis is that field experience takes place outside the classroom in actual sport business settings. Case study takes place inside the classroom. The two methods complement each other. In case study, the students learn from situations that may or may not be real. Therefore, if mistakes are made, they can be corrected without consequences to a real sport business. The students are guided by the instructor toward better thinking, analyzing, and developing solutions.

In many sport marketing courses, students practice the fundamentals of sport marketing using case study. A case puts forth sport marketing circumstances in a particular situation in a sport business. A case might involve one sport marketing element and a single product, or many elements and issues and an entire company. The student's task is to analyze the factors and issues, develop appropriate courses of action or strategies, estimate possible consequences, and determine a best strategy or plan of action.

Case study provides the student experience in wrestling with a variety of problems and issues, honing analytical skills, explaining and defending assessments, and formulating strategies that are feasible and that should work. Many times, cases used in the classroom are presented without a complete set of facts. This is a more realistic portrayal of the real world. The purpose for this is to encourage students to develop some realistic assumptions about the incomplete information and the situation presented. This becomes a part of the student's assessment of the situation and eventually may become part of the proposed course of action.

Objectives of Case Study

The primary objective of using case studies in sport marketing is to provide classroom experience in which the student may apply the theory and principles of sport marketing to simulated sport business situations. In using case analysis, emphasis should be placed on the process of analylzing situation and arriving at decisions, not the final decision. The student should understand this and should not expect to be trying to find a "right answer or solution."

The process includes conducting research and the objective critical analysis of various information. The student learns the process with the guidance of the sport marketing course instructor. Through this practice the student will form an analytical and decision-making framework for approaching a situation, analyzing it, and formulating decisions and solution strategies.

Perhaps the greatest objective of case study is to teach the student to think critically and independently. Of course, the student must be given the full opportunity to develop that skill. The instructor provides a decision-making framework. The student uses the framework to identify problems, if there are any. Then, the student uses the framework to analyze the situation, begin to formulate possible strategies for handling the situation, identify the consequences of those strategies, and determine a best course of action.

If the instructor provides too much direction, the student will simply follow the instructor toward the answers. The student must be allowed to develop work on a case completely even if the instructor knows that the student's plan will not work. Afterward the instructor should point out to the student the weaknesses and strengths of the plan, why they are weaknesses and strengths, and why it most likely is not the best plan of action. In most cases the student's plan is not one that will not work at all. It might be that the student's plan is one that has too many weaknesses or one that will create ineffective or negative consequences to work effectively and successfully. This teaches the student to predict the possible consequences of the solutions.

In trying to predict consequences of solutions, the student tries to determine if, how, and why something will or will not work best for a given situation and what will be the effect of the solutions on people, the environment, or other factors. Based on these predictions the student may make changes in order to strengthen the plan of action or in order to impact the effect the actions may have on people, the environment, or other factors.

Case study requires a lot of work from the student and the instructor. Each must come to the class well prepared in order to effect success. Case study requires that the student become an analytical thinker, and this can be demanding. The student must learn how to determine if problems exist in a case, formulate objectives from which a solution plan will be developed, predict outcomes and consequences, change parts of the plan if needed, and defend decisions and strategies.

It requires the instructor to be a guide, not a lecturer with all the answers. The instructor must allow the student to think independently and yet appropriately question the student's decisions as a means of helping the student foresee the consequences of decisions. This brings reality into the classroom. The student is required to think and act as a responsible employee faced with a real problem.

On the other hand, case study does not replace actual work experience, nor should case study be regarded as a means of providing a student with all of the tools needed to analyze and solve problems. The student is preparing for the day she or he holds a fully responsible professional position in the sport industry. The skills developed in sport marketing case study — research methods, critical analysis, consequence analysis, and strategy development — are critical tools to take into the sport business industry.

Purposes of Case Study in Sport Marketing

Theory is merged into reality. The case study method offers an opportunity to apply classroom theory and fundamentals to case situations in order to test one's understanding of the theory and to determine its usefulness. The case study method allows the testing of ideas that look good in theory, but might not be practical in an actual situation. Students will draw from their knowledge of theories and fundamentals gained from courses in sport management and sport marketing to analyze the situations and develop strategies.

Attention is focused on the multiple factors and issues that can influence decisions. The case study method focuses attention on the infinite variety of goals, problems, facts, conditions (internal and external), conflicts, and personalities that exist in sport industry businesses and organizations. The student must determine what these factors and issues are in a particular case, give them consideration in analysis of the problems in a situation, and give them consideration when developing plans and strategies.

Critical thinking and decision-making abilities are developed. Critical thinking involves objective analysis. In case study, the student is required to study situations objectively and without jumping to conclusions, determine if problems exist, identify and analyze them in order to determine the root of the problems, recommend specific actions to be taken to correct or improve the situation, analyze and forecast the possible consequences of decisions, and determine a way to evaluate the entire situation and solutions.

The student should learn not to jump to conclusions. This requires the student to develop patience until the situation can be studied. Case study helps the student develop the ability to suspend making a decision until a full understanding of the situation has been developed, all elements that may be affected have been identified, all facts — directly and indirectly related — have been gathered, all consequences of any course of action have been predicted, the best course of action for that situation and for that time has been selected, and all was done in an educated and objective manner.

This helps the student develop intellectual and emotional poise.

Sport marketing elements are identified and utilized in the decision-making process. The cases used in this book vary in content, cover a variety of sport industry settings and products, and involve a variety of issues. Some of these are sport marketing research, consumer analysis, product management, pricing, organizational structure, promotional methods, leadership issues, cultural diversity issues, legal issues, and distribution. Most of the cases involve more than one element and issue. This helps the student develop the ability to identify which marketing elements are involved. This then helps the student to develop educated strategies.

Objectivity, sensitivity, and professional ethics are developed. Today's society consists of people with great diversity in lifestyles, race, values, opinions, age, handicap, and many other elements. Additionally, there are many issues and concerns in society that bring about heated debate. It is important to understand that personal beliefs, attitudes, or values toward an issue or a person may influence decisions, and that those decisions will have either a negative or positive impact. Therefore, the student should be certain that those decisions reflect attention to law, discrimination, professional ethics, and other considerations. Through case study, students can begin to develop objectivity, sensitivity, and a code of professional ethics that will help guide them in developing strategies and making decisions.

Help for the Student

Working with cases can be fun and challenging. It can also be frustrating. Let's talk about the enjoyable and challenging side of case study first. While you, the student, assume the role of a sport marketing director, or an associated role, you are given a free hand to study the case, try to discover and unlock any problems in the case, and to develop strategies about how to correct or radically change a situation according to what you believe will work. This freedom takes some time to get used to. In most all other courses, you sit and take lecture notes with the purpose of memorizing them for an exam. In using case study, there are practically no lecture notes to memorize. The purpose of case study is to teach you to think, to analyze critically and objectively, and to develop decisions and strategies that will work best for a particular situation.

There is no one correct answer in case study. There are different ideas, solutions, and strategies that can work effectively. In each situation, you develop a plan of action that will probably work best for that situation and will probably reach the objectives you formulated. There are many facts, issues, and other factors to be considered in a case. There are almost always people involved. It is your job to analyze the situation, determine if there are problems needing attention, formulate objectives that will guide you through developing a plan of action, and develop solutions or a plan of action that will work best for that particular situation.

Your plan should be discussed and analyzed by the instructor and the class. Through this process, you will learn whether or not your idea will work. If it is found that the idea will not work very well, this does not mean that it is a wrong answer, it is just one that will not work very well for that particular situation. This, of course, is when the process becomes frustrating. You believe you have uncovered all the problems in a case. You spend countless hours putting together what you believe is the greatest plan around. You believe the plan is perfect. Then your bubble is popped! The instructor or other students in the course point out that a few of the problems you uncovered are not really problems needing immediate attention. You missed the most pertinent problems in the case. Others also point out that some of your solution objectives are self-serving and will probably offend a particular population. Finally, they question the solution strategies on which you worked very hard. They point out that a few of these strategies will have more negative consequences than positive and that it would be best that you drop those strategies and develop different ones.

You must remember in these situations that the instructor and the other students are not attacking you personally! Therefore, do not throw away your work. Make notes on what others have discussed about your work. Listen to them and seriously consider their perspectives and ideas. Remember this: After one case study, you simply are not going to be able to think as critically and completely as you will after you have worked on many case studies. In other words, with lots of practice, you will learn to identify most of the problems in a case and how your decisions will affect various populations, to think of many more solution options from which to choose, and to predict the consequences of your plans.

In addition, you will learn that your work will go through many changes. Initially, this is hard to take. People tend to be afraid of change. This is because we spend so much time trying to get everything around us set in some sensible order and never change it. We also tend to think that change is weakness. Further, we are conditioned to make decisions based on our own personal beliefs, preferences, prejudices, and ideas about what is right and wrong. Keep in mind that this is exactly what you should not do. For example, think about what would happen if a judge were to use her or his personal religious beliefs in making decisions in the courtroom. Of course, this does not mean that you must change your personal beliefs. It means that as a professional person in a position making decisions that will affect a company, employees, customers, and many other things you must try your best to make sure those decisions are entirely objective, the best and most appropriate for that situation. In that capacity, you carry the responsibility for the consequences of your decisions. Therefore, it is in your best interest to make decisions that are best and appropriate and will have mostly positive consequences. When you consider making changes to your plans in this context, you will realize that change is better. Your plan will be stronger, better, and a more appropriate plan for that situation.

Group Work

There should be assignments in which you will work on a case or a project with a group. Learning to work with a group is important. There will be many times in your career in which you will work with a group or a team. In a real workplace, groups are given official titles like committees, task forces, or commissions. You should capitalize on the opportunity to experience group work and learn how to work in a group.

The first skill you must learn when working with a group is listening. You have a responsibility to listen. You never know when someone will have the idea that will be the best idea for a case. Therefore, rule number one is that you should take each person in your group seriously. This can be tough to do. There will certainly be individuals in your group with whom you disagree on many points, who is different from you in many ways, who simply gets on your nerves, or any number of factors. You must be intelligent enough and professional enough to leave those factors outside the group project. Stay professional and objective.

There will be a different perspective about a case from each individual in the group. Listen to each one. A single individual simply cannot think of every possible perspective, idea, solution idea, objective, or other factor to consider in a case. Each perspective will help you obtain a better and more complete understanding about the case. Each will help you understand how ideas and decisions can affect people in different ways. Through this process, the end result will be a project that is stronger than many projects completed by a single individual.

Another rule of group work is that each person in the group must participate equally. Actually this will practically be impossible as each person's characteristics are different, and some will contribute more work than others will. However, it never hurts to try. Try to learn what each person's skills are and how those skills can be best utilized in the group to complete the task. Do not be afraid to communicate your thoughts, ideas, and perspective about any item being discussed in the group. Encourage others to do the same.

Another goal of group work is for the group to learn how to organize a group, manage a group, assign tasks within the group, and keep the group on the right track. You will notice that in a group some individuals will tend to take charge more easily and more often than others. There are advantages and disadvantages to this. An advantage is that there is someone in the group with natural management skill. That is good for the group. There is someone who will manage the group. A disadvantage is that this person might not be the appropriate leader for the group or for the project. Some-one must recognize this and move to change the leader. Another disadvantage is that if one person is always taking charge, then others never have a chance to be the leader. Again, someone must recognize this and specifi-cally appoint those individuals who need the practice.

Communication

Communication is very important. If you cannot communicate your ideas, thoughts, suggestions, or critical analyses, no one will understand what you are trying to say. Therefore, you must learn to communicate orally and in writing. Oral communication is usually very different from commu-nication in writing. Writing typically requires proper English grammar and composition and correct spelling. In your career, there will be plenty of times when you will be required to prepare reports or projects in writing. Imagine what your boss will think about you if you cannot communicate your ideas, if your English is poor, or if you can not spell correctly. The time to learn to communicate is now, not when you are on the job.

The skills of negotiation and persuasion as forms of communication are important. You already possess these skills although they are probably very limited. For example, have you ever argued with a parent to raise your al-lowance? Have you ever tried to convince a friend to see a particular movie even though the friend has stubbornly refused? In these conversations, you most likely used a number of arguments and reasons why your proposal should be accepted. Now it is time for you to improve those skills. In case study, consider your arguments and reasons that will support your ideas. Develop those reasons that show why you have made particular decisions. Use research and communication skills to make your arguments stronger.

Research

Don't be afraid of the word "research." Research does not always mean setting up an elaborate study and conducting it for a long period of time. It also does not always mean spending countless hours in a library reading everything there. Research, in its most rudimentary forms, involves experimenting, investigating, studying, exploring, examining, gathering information, and searching for answers. As a sport marketer you will be conducting research. Your research will involve many methods depending on your purpose: conducting surveys, conducting consumer analysis, test marketing a product, searching for information to support a marketing proposal to the boss, and many other forms.

You should use research in case study. The information you find for a case will help you develop stronger strategies. For example, if there are legal matters to attend to in a case, you could seek help from an attorney, or you could go to a law library and find information there that would help. The result is that you have researched for answers or for data and found what you needed, and the information becomes a strong part of your case.

The Instructor's Role

Teaching with case studies can be fun. Keep in mind that this approach is definitely challenging. You now enter into an instructor-student relationship that is different from lecture-only classes because using case studies is different from delivering lectures.

The atmosphere you will develop in the classroom is very important. The atmosphere must be one that is nonthreatening to any student. This can be done by establishing rules to which the students must adhere when participating in discussion, group work, and individual work. The students must be encouraged to be open and forthright with their ideas. It is a scary moment for most students when they present their work for analysis. They are afraid of failure, nonacceptance, mockery, or other factors. You must establish an atmosphere that is open, accepting of, and objective about each student's work. The student must know that no idea is a stupid idea. It could possibly be the very best idea, or it is simply one that is not the best for that particular situation.

The student will ask you for the right answers. You must be prepared to help the student understand why you believe the idea is not right for that particular situation. This involves analyzing and predicting the effects or consequences of the student's ideas. All decisions have consequences, and most have both positive and negative consequences. Point out those positive and negative consequences.

You might feel an overwhelming urge to tell your students what you would do in the cases. The students might beg you to tell them. Remember, most of the students are looking for what you would do because they believe the instructor's solution is the "right" one. Therefore, if the student learns how you would approach a situation and how you tend to develop solutions for the situations, that is exactly what they will try to copy.

Keep in mind that sometimes you might be wrong about your analysis of a student's work. Therefore, do not judge a student's plan too quickly. Always allow the student plenty of time to discuss the reasoning behind decisions and actions. Allow time for a discussion of the student's predictions of the consequences of the plan. You will find that for every student in your class there will be that many ideas about what to do in a situation.

Keep in mind that the case study method of learning is not an infallible one. The direction and guidance you offer will have a profound effect on the student's developing attitude and professionalism. It is important, therefore, that you make every effort to use the case study method in an appropriate manner. You must take an objective role and allow the student to present her or his arguments in full, after which, you and the student should analyze the student's work for strengths and weaknesses in light of appropriate actions, ethical actions, and actions and strategies that are best for the situation presented.

Philosophies and attitudes the student learns throughout the case study experience will most likely stay with the students well into their first job. This experience undoubtedly increases the student's capacity to approach a situation, analyze it effectively and finally to develop objectives and strategies for action if needed. In this approach you must guide the student in such a way that she or he arrives at decisions through careful and objective analysis: the examining and reexamining of all the facts and other information pertinent to the situation.

Group Work

One goal of case study should be to develop the ability to work in a group. The objective here should be to teach the student to learn to listen to others in a group, organize and assign tasks, and work effectively with others. Therefore, use some case studies as group projects. Discuss the importance of learning to work in a group. Develop some guidelines for working in a group. Develop a method for evaluating each individual's contribution to the group work.

Communication

Communication is important. The student must learn to communicate orally and in writing. Develop assignments and projects that require the student to communicate orally and in writing. For example, use assignments and activities in which the student must make oral presentations and assignments and activities that require the student to perform written tasks with the case studies.

Find ways to develop the student's ability to negotiate and to persuade. The skills of negotiation and persuasion are important to the sport marketer. Communication and research are the necessary skills to be effective at negotiation and persuasion. Encourage the student's use of these skills. Develop assignments and activities that require the use of them.

Research

Research is important in sport marketing. The student must learn to do research. Finding answers and information is necessary for a sport marketer to do a successful job. Encourage research with the cases as a means of obtaining information, using information, and supporting decisions.

Suggested Further Reading

Bannon, J. J., & Busser, J. A. (1992). *Problem solving in recreation and parks.* Champaign, IL: Sagamore Publishing Inc.

Culkin, D. F., & Kirsch, S. L. (1986). *Managing human resources in recreation, parks, and leisure services.* New York: Macmillan Publishing Company.

DeSensi, J. T., & Rosenberg, D. (1996). *Ethics in sport management.* Morgantown, WV: Fitness Information Technology, Inc.

Kraus, R. (1994). *Leisure in a changing America: Multicultural perspectives.* New York: Macmillan Publishing Company.

Moody, P. E. (1983). *Decision making.* New York: McGraw-Hill Book Company.

Pitts, B. G., & Stotlar, D. K. (1996). *Fundamentals of sport marketing.* Morgantown, WV: Fitness Information Technology, Inc.

Thoma, J. E., & Chalip, L. (1996). *Sport governance in the global community.* Morgantown, WV: Fitness Information Technology, Inc.

Zeigler, E. F. (1982). *Decision-making in physical education and athletics administration: A case method approach.* Champaign, IL: Stipes Publishing Company.

CHAPTER 2

A Strategic Sport Marketing
Case Analysis Model

Overview of the Strategic Sport Marketing Case Analysis Model

The strategic sport marketing case analysis model presented in this book is the result of many years of searching for the complete case analysis model. It was developed from various case analysis models (see the "Suggested Reading" section at the end of this chapter)

The strategic sport marketing case analysis model presented here consists of three phases (see Figure 1). In Phase One, Situation Analysis and Problem Identification, the student must examine the situation, determine if problems exist, and identify those problems. In Phase Two, Sport Marketing Analysis, the consumer and product markets must be analyzed. Phase Three is the Marketing Program Development. In Phase Three, solution objectives are formulated, and strategies and plans of action are developed.

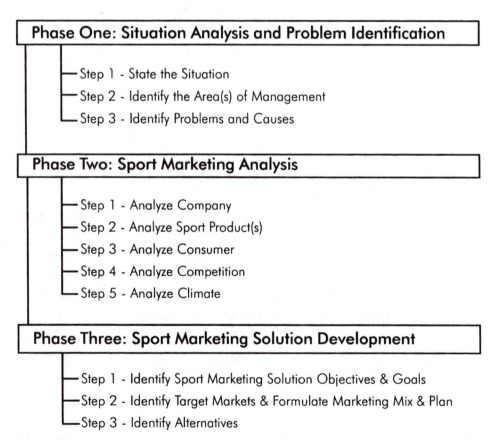

Figure 1
Sport marketing case analysis model

You should study the model to understand the complete model and each of its steps. Practice using the model on a case or two. If you find it hard to remember some of the sport marketing concepts you learned in sport marketing class, take out your notes from that class and your textbook, and refer to them when needed.

In some cases you may not be able to apply every step. Remember that the cases vary in length, situation, and the amount and type of information given. In this situation you are expected to make educated assumptions about the missing information. That is, it is not a good analysis to simply state that the information is missing. The good analysis will point out that certain information is missing and will make intelligent assumptions about the voids.

Phase One:
Situation Analysis
and Problem Identification

The first step in analyzing a given situation is to examine the facts, evidence and all other pertinent information available. If you determine there are problems, then you must determine the underlying root of the problems.

One of the purposes of Phase One is for you to learn how to seek and identify the facts in a given situation. You should not make immediate conclusions or assumptions without all of the facts. You will learn how to recognize all of the facts pertinent to a situation in order to make educated decisions.

Another purpose of Phase One is for you to learn to analyze a situation according to specific factors in order to determine if there are any problems. Do not assume that there are problems just because you are given a case to analyze. Analysis means that one must examine and reexamine the entire situation from all angles and from all viewpoints, consider the damages, identify the consequences, and determine if these are really problems that need correcting.

Remember that every situation is unique. The facts, information available, people involved, and other factors within any given sport business situation can be different from other situations. You may draw upon past situations and experience and study the analysis and decisions made in those cases that are similar to a present situation. This will help in analyzing and developing strategies and solutions for problems. There is, however, a danger in referring to how you solved a prior problem. The danger arises when the problem solver does not study the new situation, compare it to the old one, and analyze it properly. The necessary time to study the new situation is not taken, and a quick and easy answer is given: "Let's do that again. It worked the first time."

Another method that is helpful to analyze and develop solutions is to study other businesses and what strategies are being used. A sport marketer should always study other businesses, sport and nonsport. There may be strategies that will work for the company or solutions that will work for your problems. Another reason for studying your competition is to understand them. You may use this knowledge in many different ways to help your success.

The intelligent decision maker will not simply apply a solution plan from a prior situation even though it may be the easy way out. The extra amount of time spent to properly analyze a situation and arrive at educated decisions can often be the difference between success and failure.

One approach to analyzing and solving problems is to hire a sport marketing consultant. This, of course, will cost money and in some cases, quite a bit of money. The knowledge gained from a sport marketing case study course will not give all the answers but should provide an analytical framework that may be used in most problem situations. Using that framework as a foundation you will have a basic knowledge with which to approach a situation.

There are three steps in Phase One. Study each one carefully. Discuss it with your instructor and other students in class in order to understand it thoroughly before using it.

Step 1: State the Situation. The purpose of Step 1 is to study and understand a situation. You will objectively identify all the pertinent facts, people, and other factors in a situation. You must seek to really understand what has happened, what might happen, who is involved, and the personalities of those involved. Resist the temptation to proclaim you already know the problems in a case. You have only just begun to get to know the case.

In Step 1 you will act as a detective. You will gather all the facts and evidence in the case. You will study the case until you can state the situation in your own words. Here are some ideas on working through Step 1.

Read the case several times. Make notes about certain facts and information given and about information you believe is missing. Describe the situation in your own words orally and in writing. Read the case again. Check your description of the case with the actual case again. Add to it if needed. Do not identify any problems at this point.

Identify any and all marketing elements readily apparent in the situation, such as, research, product, price, place, and promotion strategies given, product development, and market or industry analysis.

Step 2: Identify the Area(s) of Management. Determining what management areas the situation falls into will help you determine problems and will help you develop solutions for those problems. This guides you to resources that may be used if needed. It also guides you to the individuals within those management areas on whom you might need to call for help either in identifying problems and/or in determining solutions for the problems. Does the situation seem to be a legal one? Might it be a personnel one? Has the situation come about because of something in the area of facilities? Is it a pricing strategy situation? There are also other areas of management and marketing to consider, such as program management, distribution, consumer behavior, advertising, product policy, legislation, and licensing.

Once you have identified the areas within which you believe the situation falls, identify resources available. For example, if one area is personnel management, a resource you will probably want to use is the personnel policy manual. If the situation seems to fall into the new product development area, you will want to know what the company policies are on new product development and who works on those policies.

Step 3: Identify Problems and Causes. It is now time to try to determine if there are any problems in the case, what the problems are and the causes of those problems. First refer to your work in Step 1. Ask this question: What brought about this situation? Your answers to this question will be your first list of problems for the case. Now ask this question about each problem you listed: Is this really a problem? The answer to that is whether or not the situation brought about is a negative one or a positive one. If the situation is negative for the company or for the people involved, then you have a situation in which something needs to be addressed. If it seems to be a positive one, then perhaps nothing needs to be changed.

Ask many more questions about the situation. For every question you ask, ask an opposite question. For example, if you ask this question, Why didn't sales of the new golf clubs increase in May?, an opposite question would be Why did new golf club sales increase in months other than May?

For every problem you identify, consider the opposite. In other words, do not be satisfied with one line of questioning or examination. Ask questions or cross-examine from another perspective. This will help you to see many more sides of the situation and will help you to really uncover the real problems and causes of those problems.

The purpose for identifying the causes of problems is that herein lies the real root of the problem. If the root of the problem is not corrected, then the problem is likely to recur. Do everything you can to uncover the causes of your list of problems. These are the factors for which your solutions will be developed.

Phase Two: Sport Marketing Analysis

After thorough analysis and discussion of a situation to the point that you are satisfied and you have identified objectively the problems and causes in a situation, it is time to analyze the situation from a marketing perspective. This is done after the situation analysis because you must understand the situation from an overall perspective first and then from a marketing perspective. Keep in mind that marketing is only one facet of an organization and must not be considered in a vacuum. All areas of a company are linked.

After identifying the problems in a case, you will analyze the case from a marketing perspective. This is done after determining the problems because it will help you make educated decisions concerning solutions for the case.

Step 1: Analyze the Company. Analyze the company or organization according to the following: history, growth of company, location, population, number of employees, strengths of the company, weaknesses of the company, and financial situation and financial resources.

Step 2: Analyze the Sport Product(s). List and describe the sport product(s) offered by the company or organization. Describe the products' functions, utilities, and benefits. Identify the current and historical product life cycle stages. Identify the sport industry segment according to the Pitts, Fielding, & Miller (1994) model (refer to the appendix). Describe the strengths and weaknesses of the product(s). Describe the present price and cost structure.

Step 3: Analyze the Consumer. Identify the consumer markets the company targets currently. Describe them in detail (if given in the case). Describe the nature of the demand for the company's existing products. Describe the extent of demand. Describe the strengths and weaknesses of the current markets. Identify potential new markets.

Step 4: Analyze the Competition. Identify the competition and describe them in detail. Estimate the number of competitors and their market shares, financial resources, and marketing resources. Describe the strengths and weaknesses of the competition. Identify potential future competition.

Step 5: Analyze the Climate. Identify environmental factors affecting the situation, such as social, legal, and political environments. Discuss the possibility of future changes in environmental factors that might affect the situation.

Phase Three:
Sport Marketing Solution Development

The development of solution objectives and the marketing plan is the final phase in the case analysis model.

Step 1: Identify Sport Marketing Solution Objectives and Goals. You will need to consider if you need objectives that are long-range, short-range and stop-gap. Long-range objectives might be objectives that could take a year or 10 years to complete. Short-range objectives might take a month or more. Stop-gap objectives exist to remedy a situation immediately until other short — or long-range solution objectives can be developed.

How will you know which type of objectives you need? There is no specific formula. Objectives are developed out of how you want to solve problems and what you want to accomplish through those solutions.

Based on your complete analysis of the situation, the problems and their causes, what do you want to accomplish through your solutions for this case? Do you simply want to remedy a problem, or do you want to go further and turn the problem into a new opportunity for the company? Is it a problem that requires a stop-gap solution? Are the problems ones that require complex solutions and quite a length of time to pursue? What will you need in order to pursue solution objectives you set? Do you have those resources? If not, how might you obtain them?

Before moving on to the next step, you should consider the possible consequences of your solution objectives. This is difficult to do. Try to predict the outcome of your objectives based on the problems and the situation of the company. What can you estimate will be the positive consequences, and what will be the negative consequences? For example, a positive consequence is that a particular solution objective will be achieved. A negative consequence of the same objective is that you might lose a particular consumer segment. Now consider the impact of each of the consequences. What are the overall advantages and disadvantages of each of the consequences for the company in many respects? You might decide that the negative consequence will not have a great impact on the company. Therefore, the solution objective is one that will mostly positively affect the company. Your decision is to keep the objective.

Step 2: Identify Target Market(s), Formulate Marketing Mix and Marketing Plan. Not every one of your sport marketing problems will require a complete sport marketing plan. However, if your solution objectives calls for changing a marketing plan or creating a new one, then you must know the process of developing a marketing plan.

After making final decisions on your marketing solution objectives, it is time to identify your target market(s) and to develop the marketing mix and marketing plan. These decisions should be based on your objectives. This is the plan of action to be used to achieve your objectives.

Your first step is to identify your target market(s). This may already exist if you are working within an existing marketing plan. If not, this process begins with the identification of your consumer market segments. If you don't remember how to do this, refer to material from your sport marketing class and textbook.

Your next step is to develop the marketing mix: product, price, promotion, and place. Make your decisions based on your objectives and target markets. Again, if you need help, refer to your sport marketing class notes and textbook.

After making decisions on your marketing mix components, plan strategies for the achievement of them. Your strategies should include decisions on factors such as, but not limited to, time schedules, financial resources available, financial resources attainment, people needed to work on the plan, work schedules, other materials needed, deadlines, contracts, licensing if needed, and legal counsel if needed.

You now should try to predict the consequences of your plan of action. Just as you did for your objectives, try to determine what the positive and negative consequences of these actions will be for your consumer and your company. If necessary, change segments of your plan until you reach a point that you are satisfied with the consequences and the effect on the consumer and the company.

Step 3: Identify Alternatives. Do not throw away all of the ideas you developed earlier. Keep those ideas. You might be able to use them as alternatives if something goes wrong with your original plan. In other words, this step can be thought of as Plan B to back up Plan A if it does not work as you anticipated.

Suggestions for Activities and Assignments

Each instructor who uses case studies has most likely developed an individual style for this method of instruction, has probably developed case studies, and might have a variety of activities and assignments that she or he uses with case studies. If you are that instructor, the following activities and assignments are offered to add to your possibilities. For those instructors who are using case studies for the first time, the following activities and assignments and the case analysis model will help you have an easier start.

Questions. For each case, there is a set of questions that may be used in many ways. Here are a few examples: Choose specific questions or use all of them; discuss the questions in class; divide the class into groups and have each group discuss the questions; have the groups discuss one or two of the questions and present their discussion to the class; assign the questions as an out-of-class written assignment; use the questions as exam study guides; use the questions as exam questions.

Use the case analysis model in a variety of ways. Here are a few suggestions: Have the students apply only one phase of the model; use selected steps of the model; assign a case for out-of-class analysis, and have the students turn in a written analysis of the case using the model; use the model in class for analysis and discussion; use the model for the final exam; have the students give oral presentations of their analysis with the model.

Use the case analysis model as the framework for the semester. There are three phases in the model. Use one phase for the first third of the semester, the second phase for the second third, and the third phase for the last third. During the second third of the semester, the student uses both Phases One and Two. In the last third of the semester, use all three. This gives the student time to master one phase at a time.

Team Projects. Divide the class into small teams. Have the teams use the model or certain parts of the model with a case. Have each team present its work to the class for analysis.

Role Play. Choose a case you believe will lend itself well for role play. Assign parts and roles. Have the students act out the case and their solutions in class.

Other outside assignments. Ask the student to find a sport industry case study in another marketing case book and bring it to class for discussion.

Develop a list of basic marketing questions. Ask the students to find and bring to class sport magazine or newspaper articles about the sport industry. Use the list of questions in number 4 below to discuss the article from a sport marketing perspective. Sample questions might include:

- What is the sport product discussed in the article?
- Are the consumer markets discussed? If so, who are they? If not, what do you believe they are?
- Are marketing or advertising or promotions discussed in the article? If so, identify them.
- Do you believe these promotions are appropriate for the product and the consumer? If not, what would you do?
- Who are the competitors?
- What is the sport industry segment?
- What is the nature of this segment?

Brief Case Analysis for Small Group Work. In class, this activity is best used at the beginning of the semester (or quarter) as a lead-up activity for later in-depth case study. Following are the steps for the activity:

1. Prior to the class, select cases. The number of cases will depend on how many groups you will establish, how many cases you want each group to discuss, and if you want each group to use the same case or different cases. The time needed for this is approximately 75–90 minutes. (As an incentive for thorough discussion, have each group give a presentation of their case and discussion. This usually takes about 5 to 10 minutes per group.)
2. Establish groups of 4 to 5 and assign a leader of each group.
3. The students should have their sport marketing course notes and text available for reference during the discussion.
4. Give the following list of discussion questions to each member of each group, and begin.

(1)

Briefly describe the sport business/organization. Include business type, company location, and general background information about the business.

(2)

Are business objectives given? What are they? Discuss.

(3)

Who are the consumer target markets? Discuss the demographics and psychographics of the consumer markets for this company.

(4)

What is (are) the product(s) offered by this company (product market and industry analysis)? What is (are) the product line(s)? What are the product items in the product line(s)? Analyze all facets of the product(s), such as what function does(do) the product(s) fulfill for the consumer?

(5)

Determine which sport industry segment the product(s) may be categorized as (refer to the appendix).

(6)

Discuss the demand for these products. What is the market share of this company?

(7)

What are internal and external factors in the sport industry segment that might affect the business?

(8)

What are the prices for the products? What are the pricing strategies? Do you believe the product will sell for the set price?

(9)

What is the distribution system of the company? Is it effective? Would you suggest another distribution strategy?

(10)

What are the promotional mix and promotional strategies of the company?

(11)

Do you see any opportunities or problems of the company in this situation? What are the factors you believe are causing the problems? Discuss the problems and opportunities and discuss possible solutions for them.

(12)

What is your complete analysis of this company and your solutions for its problems/opportunities?

References and Suggested Reading

Bannon, J. J. (1987). *Problem solving in recreation and parks.* Champaign, IL: Management Learning Laboratories.

Bannon, J. J., & Busser, J. A. (1992). *Problem solving in recreation and parks.* Champaign, IL: Sagamore Publishing Inc.

Bernhardt, K. L. & Kinnear, T. C. (1985). *Cases in marketing management.* Plano, TX: Business Publications, Inc.

Pitts, B. G., & Fielding, L. W. (1991). Strategic sport marketing: Case analysis. In Parkhouse, B. L. (Ed.), *The management of sport: Its foundation and application.* St. Louis: Mosby Year Book.

Zeigler, E. F. (1982). *Decision-making in physical education and athletics administration: A case method approach.* Champaign, IL: Stipes Publishing Company.

PART II

• • • • • • • • • • • •

The Cases

How the Sport Marketing Case Studies Are Organized

Case study does not require that the case studies be organized or categorized in any particular method. However, it is common that case studies are organized in some manner to help the instructor and student in using the cases in a more productive way. In marketing, case study textbooks sometime organize the cases according to marketing tasks, such as promotion, pricing, or distribution. Some are organized according to type of industry, such as service industry, entertainment industry, or music industry.

The case studies in this book are organized according to research involving sport industry segmentation. In their study, Pitts, Fielding, and Miller (1994) suggest that the sport industry can be divided into three industry segments: the sport performance industry segment, the sport production industry segment, and the sport promotion industry segment. Pitts et al. argue that all products in or related to the sport business industry can be categorized into one of these three segments. Understanding the sport industry as a whole and in parts — industry segments — can provide guidance for the sport administrator in decision making. The sport marketer must understand product functions, utility, and benefits to be able to truly give the consumer what the consumer wants. Read the study provided in the appendix in order to understand the segments. In addition, study chapter 8 in the Pitts and Stotlar (1996) textbook for a better understanding of product functions, utility, and benefits.

The cases are divided into three sections. The sections are titled by the three sport industry segments as developed in the Pitts, Fielding, & Miller Industry Segment Model (1994). The purposes for using a research study as a framework for this book are to apply research to the industry and to provide a guideline to ensure that you have opportunity to work on a variety of sport business case studies. The article and model are reprinted in the Appendix. You will want to refer to it often.

This book is also written to be a companion book to *Fundamentals of Sport Marketing* (Pitts & Stotlar, 1996). You will want to use the principles of sport marketing in working on the cases. You may also want to use other textbooks specific to sport marketing and sport management as references. There are some selected ones in the sections titled "Suggested Reading" at the end of each case.

References

Pitts, B. G., Fielding, L. W., & Miller, L. K. (1994). Industry segmentation theory and the sport industry: Developing a sport industry segment model. *Sport Marketing Quarterly, 3* (1), 15–24.

Pitts, B. G., & Stotlar, D. K. (1996). *Fundamentals of sport marketing.* Morgantown, WV: Fitness Information Technology.

SECTION 1

THE SPORT PERFORMANCE INDUSTRY SEGMENT

The Sport Performance Industry Segment: An Overview

In this segment of the industry, sports performance is the product for sale. Sports performance products include sports, recreation, leisure, and fitness activities. These all have one thing in common: They are activity products. Activity products in the sport industry are sold to consumers in two broad categories: participation and spectatorial.

The consumer can purchase participation products including participating in a basketball tournament, joining a fitness center to work out, hiking in the Himalayas, scuba diving at Cozumel, camping in the Smokey Mountains, canoeing on the Mississippi River, and running in a marathon. All of these products are participation products.

The product for sale is sport performance as a participation product. The sport marketer selling this product must understand the special product attributes of participation in order to enhance success of properly promoting the product and selling it. People participate in sports for many reasons, some of which are fun, recreation, entertainment, competition, social, love of the sport, fitness, and weight maintenance or weight reduction. Therefore, as with any other product, if sport marketers understand these product functions, they can communicate more effectively through advertising and other promotional methods to enhance their chances of selling the product. To see this in practice, find advertisements for fitness centers in your local newspaper. Read them and notice the language used in the ads. Do you see any of the product functions mentioned here, such as lose weight, get in shape, have fun, meet people?

Sport performance is also sold in a very different way in the sport industry. It can be sold as an entertainment, or spectatorial, product. Some of these include college soccer matches, body-building contests, and basketball games. Today, many sports events are created almost solely for the purpose of entertainment. Consider, for example, the American Gladiators, boxing, and men's arena football. Why would a person pay an admission fee to watch a basketball game? There are many reasons, most of which are related to entertainment. Some of these are, to have something to do, to have fun with friends, to support the team, to try to get on television, to be a part of the action, or to watch a known player perform. Therefore, the sport marketer needs to study and understand the consumer to determine why the consumer buys the product. This knowledge is used for specific marketing strategies, such as advertising, pricing, and scheduling. Again, watch for newspaper advertisements or television commercials about a sports event. You will notice the way the ad or commercial communicates to you in that it attempts to make the event attractive to you enough that you want to attend. One example to consider is the advertising for the annual Super Bowl. The marketers are trying to make the event sound appealing enough to entice you to go to the event, or at least to watch it on TV.

The common element is sport performance, and the sport marketing person must concentrate on the functions and benefits of either participating in or watching an activity. As the sport marketing person better understands the utilities, functions, and benefits of these products, chances for communicating with the consumer about the product are increased. Refer to chapter 8 in the Pitts and Stotlar (1996) textbook.

The cases in this section include two participation and three spectatorial cases. There are professional and ethical issues to consider in some cases as well as the many other marketing elements.

EVERY GAME'S A BIG EVENT: THE TOLEDO MUD HENS BASEBALL CLUB

Jacquelyn Cuneen, Bowling Green State University

Professional baseball has been played at various sites in Toledo, Ohio, since 1883. Teams had a variety of names such as White Stockings, Swamp Angels, Black Pirates, and Glass Sox. Bay View Park was the home site in 1896. Bay View was situated near a marshland that was brimming with peculiar-looking birds with short wings and long legs known as marsh hens, rails, or mud hens. The abundance of the birds near their park gave the Toledo Mud Hens Baseball Club their enduring nickname (Toledo Mud Hens Baseball Club, Inc., 1994e).

The Mud Hens are currently a beloved Toledo tradition. Residents of northwest Ohio and southeast Michigan consider the Hens to be a local treasure. Fans check Hens' scores and standings regularly; advertising signs at various fast-food restaurants and other surrounding businesses support the Hens throughout the year by posting messages related to the Hens' schedule and record; infants, children, and adults can be seen attired in Mud Hens clothing routinely; and names of Mud Hens players are as recognizable to Toledoans as those of any currently popular major league phenomenon.

The Mud Hens are one of the few minor league baseball teams to have achieved international fame. Toledo native Jamie Farr was frequently attired in a Mud Hens' cap and game shirt while portraying Maxwell Klinger on the M*A*S*H television situation comedy when the program aired regularly on CBS-TV. Currently, Farr can be seen wearing the Mud Hens clothing in M*A*S*H syndication worldwide. The team's unusual opportunities for publicity through Farr's portrayal of Klinger seem to have reaped rewards; *Baseball America* ("Reader Survey," 1994) reader survey results indicated that Mud Hens was the favorite minor league team nickname among baseball fans. The current popularity of collecting minor league baseball merchandise has also favored the Mud Hens; Rousselot (1992) identified the Hens' cap as #4 of the top 10 favorite minor league baseball caps to own. Mud Hens baseball contributes much to Toledo commerce, travel, and tourism. Many tourists traveling in the region call the Hens ticket office requesting tickets to see Klinger's favorite team.

City of Toledo Activities

Toledo, Ohio (population 332,900), is located on U. S. Routes 75 and 80/90, and State Routes 23 and 25 approximately one hour south of Detroit, Michigan, two hours west of Cleveland, and three hours north of Cincinnati. The city is situated on the western end of Lake Erie at the mouth of the Maumee (the largest river flowing into the Great Lakes). Toledo is one of the world's busiest freshwater ports and the third busiest port on the Great Lakes. The Maumee's natural harbor has 35 miles of frontage (Greater Toledo Convention and Visitors Bureau, 1994).

Toledo is predominantly an industrial city with several national manufacturing plants including Chrysler, Jeep, Libbey, Inc., Libbey-Owens-Ford, Owens-Corning, Owens-Illinois, Dana Corporation, and others. Numerous crude oil and gas pipelines are directed to Toledo, making the city a major refining center. The city is also world famous for glass production.

During the spring, summer, and autumn, when the Mud Hens play, there are several citywide events at staggered intervals, or other Toledo permanent tourist or resident attractions (Greater Toledo Convention and Visitors Bureau) that would interest groups and individuals:

1. Toledo's major annual celebration is a Rock Rhythm 'n' Blues Festival held during Memorial Day weekend. Food, beverages, games, and other activities are part of the festival.
2. An annual Northwest Ohio Rib-Off (cooking contest) is held on the waterfront in early spring. Food, beverages, games, and other activities are part of the festival.
3. Rally By the River featuring specialty foods, beverages and professional entertainment is held on the waterfront each Friday night.
4. A 2-day German-American Food Festival is held in late August.
5. Toledofest Celebration of the Arts is staged on the waterfront over Labor Day weekend. Food, beverages, games, and other activities are part of the festival.
6. Raceway Park interests many tourists and residents for harness racing events.
7. The Toledo Storm minor league hockey club (Riley Cup champion in 1993) plays at the Sports Arena from late autumn to late spring.
8. The LPGA-Jamie Farr Toledo Classic golf tournament is played at an area golf course for one week at the beginning of July.
9. The University of Toledo (UT) sponsors professional entertainment and concerts in its Glassbowl Stadium periodically. UT also conducts

an NCAA Division I sports program from late summer to late spring.

10. Fort Meigs, a reconstructed fort from the War of 1812 era, is open daily until 5:00 PM.

11. The 57-acre Toledo Botanical Gardens is open daily from 8:00 AM to 9:00 PM.

12. The Toledo Museum of Art contains more than 700 paintings by celebrated European and American artists as well as books, manuscripts, sculptures, medieval ivories, prints, tapestries, and glass. Admission to the museum is free except for special exhibits.

13. The 30-acre Toledo Zoo, containing more than 450 species of mammals, birds and reptiles in natural habitats or aquariums, is open daily from 9:00 AM to 5:00 PM.

14. The S. S. Willis B. Boyer is docked at Toledo's International Park. The Boyer is a 1911 era freighter that was the largest, most modern Great Lakes ship of its time. It is now a museum depicting freighter history and is open Wednesday to Sunday from 10:00 AM to 5:00 PM.

15. Toledo has a nationally respected symphony and ballet. Symphony and ballet seasons begin in late autumn and conclude in late spring.

16. Numerous other activities, such as ethnic festivals, riverfests, amateur theater, and various sporting activities, such as fishing, and golf are available.

Toledo's central location both as a port and major highway thoroughfare draws many travelers for overnight or extended visits. The city is also beginning to develop some distinction as a convention city. The Seagate Center is the site for larger conferences; Seagate features a 75,000 square foot exposition/trade show hall and 25 large meeting rooms.

Immediate proximity to Detroit and Cleveland sport and culture creates a natural competition for any Toledo event, and the Mud Hens understand the multiple competition rooted in both Toledo events and those originating in the surrounding area. The primary marketing objective for the Mud Hens is to maintain high attendance yearly and to continue to break the previous year's attendance records. The Hens have framed their primary marketing strategy to draw consumers by positioning baseball games in a product line that features other types of concurrent entertainment. Their theme involves making "Every Game A Big Event" for fans; each game is characterized by a special occasion or giveaway.

Product

The Mud Hens are owned by the County of Lucas, and the baseball club is a nonprofit, but self-supportive organization (i.e., no owners or share-holders gain dividends, but the baseball club must generate its own revenue in order to operate). The club is administered by a six-member board of directors (president, vice president, secretary-treasurer, two board members, and general manager) who receive no remuneration for their services. A 10-member advisory board works with the board of directors. The advisory board comprises local leaders and business executives who confer with the board of directors on various issues.

Mud Hens management consists of three assistant general managers (Community Relations, Media Relations, Ticket Operations). Other front office staff include directors for (a) marketing and entertainment, (b) marketing and sales, and (c) marketing and promotions as well as a business manager, ticket manager, clubhouse manager, head groundskeeper, stadium maintenance coordinator, and office secretary. There are various other staff positions, such as bookkeeper, public address announcer, club physician, trainer, official scorers, radio announcers, ticket manager, maintenance crew chief, and the field and coaching staff (Toledo Mud Hens Baseball Club, Inc., 1994f).

The Mud Hens' home field is Ned Skeldon Stadium located in Maumee, Ohio, a convenient suburb of Toledo. Skeldon Stadium is easily accessible from Interstate Routes 75 and 80, and State Routes 23 and 25. The stadium is 29 years old and is in excellent condition. Seating capacity is 10,025 with 2,587 box seats, 1,238 reserved seats, and 6,200 general admission seats. Skeldon Stadium has a special section designated for family seating; no alcohol is permitted in the family section. Capacity of the family section is 650.

The Hens have been a minor league farm club for five different Major League Baseball teams since their inception, but currently are an AAA team whose players are "one step away" from the Detroit Tigers. Several "name" athletes have played for the Mud Hens: Ray Chapman, Jim Thorpe, Hack Wilson, Casey Stengel, Pete Gray, Joe Niekro, Rick Cerone, Kirby Puckett, Frank Viola, Willie Hernandez, and others are Mud Hens veterans. According to *Baseball America* ("American League East," 1994a), 4 of the Tiger's top 10 future prospects currently play for the Mud Hens.

The team has been affiliated with the International League since 1965. The Hens play up to 144 games per year. All official (i.e., not exhibition) games feature other AAA opponents exclusively; teams that visit Skeldon Stadium bring numerous top 10 prospects representing their major league

affiliates. Table 1 shows International League teams, locations, and major
league affiliations (International Baseball League, 1994).

Table 1
Mud Hens Record Since 1965

Year	Wins	Losses	Percentage	Finish	Team Affiliation
1965	68	78	.466	7th	New York Yankees
1966	71	75	.486	6th	New York Yankees
1967	73	66	.525	3rd	Detroit Tigers
1968	83	64	.565	1st	Detroit Tigers
1969	68	72	.486	6th	Detroit Tigers
1970	51	89	.364	8th	Detroit Tigers
1971	60	80	.429	7th	Detroit Tigers
1972	75	69	.521	5th	Detroit Tigers
1973	65	81	.445	4th	Detroit Tigers
1974	70	74	.486	3rd	Philadelphia Phillies
1975	62	78	.443	7th	Philadelphia Phillies
1976	55	85	.393	8th	Cleveland Indians
1977	56	84	.400	8th	Cleveland Indians
1978	74	66	.529	3rd	Minnesota Twins
1979	63	76	.453	7th	Minnesota Twins
1980	77	63	.550	2nd	Minnesota Twins
1981	53	87	.379	8th	Minnesota Twins
1982	60	80	.429	7th	Minnesota Twins
1983	68	72	.486	5th	Minnesota Twins
1984	74	63	.540	3rd	Minnesota Twins
1985	71	68	.511	6th	Minnesota Twins
1986	62	77	.446	6th	Minnesota Twins
1987	70	70	.500	5th	Detroit Tigers
1988	58	84	.408	4th	Detroit Tigers
1989	69	76	.476	4th	Detroit Tigers
1990	58	86	.403	4th	Detroit Tigers
1991	74	70	.514	3rd	Detroit Tigers
1992	64	80	.444	3rd	Detroit Tigers
1993	65	77	.458	5th	Detroit Tigers

Note. Adapted from *Toledo Mud Hens 1994 Media Guide*, p. 26, by Toledo Mud
Hens Baseball Club Inc., 1994. Copyright 1994 by The Toledo Mud Hens Baseball
Club, Inc. Adapted with permission of the author.

The International League competes with two divisions: Eastern (Rochester, Ottawa, Scranton/Wilkes-Barre, Pawtucket, Syracuse) and Western (Charlotte, Richmond, Columbus, Norfolk, Toledo). The Mud Hens have posted various records against division opponents over past years (see Table 2).

Table 2
International League Teams and Major League Affiliations

Team	Location	Affiliations
Charlotte Knights	Charlotte, NC	Cleveland Indians
Columbus Clippers	Columbus, OH	New York Yankees
Norfolk Tides	Norfolk, VA	New York Mets
Ottawa Lynx	Ottawa, Ontario, Canada	Montreal Expos
Pawtucket Red Sox	Pawtucket, RI	Boston Red Sox
Richmond Braves	Richmond, VA	Atlanta Braves
Rochester Red Wings	Rochester, NY	Baltimore Orioles
Scranton/Wilkes-Barre Red Barons	Moosic, PA	Philadelphia Phillies
Syracuse Chiefs	Syracuse, NY	Toronto Blue Jays
Toledo Mud Hens	Toledo, OH	Detroit Tigers

Note. Adapted from *International League Record Book 1994*, pp. 36-73, by the International League of Professional Baseball Clubs, 1994. Copyright 1994 by International League of Professional Baseball Clubs. Adapted with permission of author.

In the past 7 years, the team has posted .500 records twice. Generally, the team plays .400 level baseball. Performance records do not appear to affect attendance substantially.

The Mud Hens have broken single-season attendance records each year since 1991 (Toledo Mud Hens Baseball Club, Inc., 1994f). Average daily attendance is 3,553; average nightly attendance is 4,271. Final figures for the 1993 season indicated that 285,155 fans attended Mud Hens baseball games.

Unique Features of Mud Hens Baseball

Numerous activities and pranks involving the fans make attendance at Mud Hens games different from attendance at other baseball games. Hens management attributes some attendance successes to unique game features that make attendance fun for spectators by involving them in high-jinks between or during baseball innings. Fans sign up at the Hens Customer Service Desk (located near the entrance gates, souvenir and concessions stands) to participate in various activities and contests such as:

Dancin' with Muddy: The Mud Hens team mascot is Muddy the Mud Hen. Muddy circulates throughout the stadium during games and randomly appears somewhere in the stands in the middle of the third inning to lead the section in a dance to a favorite tune of the day.

Homerun Inning: If the Hens hit a home run during the fourth inning, a fan whose name is drawn wins a brand-name cellular phone.

Safe at Home Dash: Children age 14 and under may be selected to race Muddy around the bases before the start of each game. If children reach home safely before Muddy, they are eligible for a drawing to win season-ticket coupon books to use the following year. The contest is sponsored by a local home security firm; Muddy has yet to win the dash.

Superfan: Fans may complete an essay of 25 words or fewer explaining why they should be the game's "Superfan." The superfan winner is announced at the end of the fifth inning; winners receive a Hens cap and T-shirt compliments of the daily Toledo newspaper.

Singers in the Stands: Fans may sign up to sing "Take Me Out to the Ballgame" during the seventh-inning stretch. A cordless microphone is delivered to their seats, and singers win free hot dogs compliments of a brand-name food distributor.

Car & Boat Race: Skeldon Stadium owns a sophisticated score and message board capable of generating unique graphics. Chad, the Hens' scoreboard operator, has achieved some local celebrity by generating creative graphics and contests. For instance, the message board shows a daily or nightly race between a car and a boat. Fans on the first-base line cheer for the car while fans on the third-base line cheer for the boat; fans behind home base cheer for a tie. Randomly selected fans on the winning side receive various products compliments of a local waste management firm.

Hens' Jukebox: Lists of songs are displayed on the message board at the end of the seventh inning, and fans cheer for the song they wish to hear. Chad's noise-meter determines the winning song according to cheers, and fans sing along with the recording.

Various other events and comical giveaways are featured. Several lotteries are held during the game using those halves of spectators' tickets that have been retained by gate attendants. When numbers are announced, spectators report to the Hens Information Desk to claim their unannounced prize. Prizes are donated by local enterprises and may include a used tire, a movie marquee poster, a bookstore display, bicycle handlebars, or numerous other whimsical prizes. Prizes and winners are displayed to the crowd via Chad's message board.

Single Game Attendance Incentives

The Mud Hens and various sponsors stage numerous promotions and giveaways (Toledo Mud Hens Baseball Club, Inc., 1994f). Giveaways range from standard to unique. Typical giveaways such as cap nights or photo nights, are sponsored by locally owned or franchised enterprises. The Mud Hens also provide humorous or useful novelties or special appearances for nearly each game. Table 3 contains a partial list of single-game incentives.

Normal ticket prices apply for all giveaway games. There is no age limit restricting the giveaway of novelties. All promotions and giveaways are advertised heavily by the Hens; Mud Hens' estimates show that giveaway sponsors are featured in advertising packages worth approximately $9,148 (Toledo Mud Hens Baseball Club, Inc., 1994c).

Famous Mascot

Muddy the Mud Hen received national-level press coverage from *Sports Illustrated* (O'Brian, 1993) when James G. Konecny, Assistant General Manager and Media Relations Director, secured a shoe contract for Muddy through a regional representative for Converse. Muddy is present for all Mud Hens games and events. The mascot moves around each section of Skeldon Stadium but always returns periodically to Muddy's Nest atop the Hens' dugout. Muddy may be armed with any number of gadgets, such as a large, plastic children's baseball bat used as a conductor's baton to prompt the crowd, or a super size water shooter used to heckle.

Muddy attends various community functions and is frequently an invited guest to local children's and adult's birthday parties. The Hens and a national-franchise ice cream retailer sponsor an annual "birthday bash" for Muddy as a pre-game event each July. Muddy's friends, including Yogi Bear and other famous characters, attend to celebrate with the fans.

Photographs of Muddy are popular in the Toledo area, especially if they are personally autographed. Muddy is also featured on a line of baseball cards that have the mascot posed in various comic or athletic positions.

Concessions and Souvenirs

Concessions and souvenir stands are located in the large concourse immediately inside the entrance gates. The Mud Hens offer traditional baseball-

Table 3
Partial Listing of Mud Hens' Special Game Incentives

Sponsor and Event	Sponsor's Origin
Mud Hens Opening Day	Local (Mud Hens)
Pepsi Night 1	Regional-National
CableSystem Night	Local
Detroit Tigers Exhibition	Local (Mud Hens)
Anderson's/Eveready Battery Night	Local-National
Martian Antenna Night	Local (Mud Hens)
Sherwin Williams Painters Caps Night	Local-National
Famous Chicken	Local (Mud Hens)
U. A .W. Night	Local
NW Ohio Chiropractor Night	Regional
Shriners' Night Parade	Regional
Friendly's-Muddy's Birthday Bash	Local-National
Detroit Tigers/Toledo Tussle	Regional (Mud Hens)
Mud Hens Banner Day	Local (Mud Hens)
Toledo Blade Reader's Night	Local
Ramada Inn Team Photo Night	Local-National
Turn Back the Clock Weekend	Local (Mud Hens)
Burger King/TV 5 Kids Clinic	Local
Manwich Cap Night	National
Famous Chicken 2	Local (Mud Hens)
Ohio Baseball Hall of Fame Induction	Regional (Mud Hens)
Baseball Card Show	Local (Mud Hens)
Food Town Family Sunday	Regional
Karaoke Night	Local (Mud Hens)
Disco Night	Local
Sports Illustrated for Kids Give-away	National
Toledo Blade "Dawn-Patrol" Carriers Day	Local
Hens Fans Appreciation Weekend	Local (Mud Hens)
Kids Club Activities	Local (Mud Hens)
Little League Parade	Local (Mud Hens)
Arrow Thru the Head Give-away	Local (Mud Hens)
Advertisers Appreciation Night	Local (Mud Hens)

Note. Adapted from 1994 Mud Hens Schedule: *Every Game's a Big Event*, p. 6 by Toledo Mud Hens Baseball Club, Inc. Copyright 1994 by The Toledo Mud Hens Baseball Club, Inc. Adapted with permission of author.

park-type foods, snacks, and beverages at two concessions stands. Mud Hens Pizza and Hens Ice Cream Sandwiches are specialty exclusive concession foods (i. e., specially blended and/or prepared ingredients) and are available only at Skeldon Stadium. Mud Hens Pizza is not sold at regional chain or independent grocery outlets. Hawkers (15–20 per game) circulate the stands with food, snacks, and beverages. Concessions are prepared and managed by a local catering firm. Prices of food and beverages at Skeldon Stadium vary but are below typical ballpark prices.

Souvenirs are sold at the Hens' Nest, a large store located in the concourse under the third-base grandstand. A full line of Mud Hens clothing, accessories, and novelties is available; Detroit Tiger merchandise is also sold. Prices of clothing and other souvenirs are comparable to typical ballpark prices.

Mud Hens merchandise is also sold by local retailers (chain and local department stores, discount stores, convenience stores, specialty shops, and so forth). The Hens have no merchandise catalog, but do produce a product and price listing of merchandise for mail-order customers. Information is sent upon customer request; there is no mailing list.

Place

Skeldon Stadium is part of the 180-acre Lucas County Recreation Center complex. The Toledo Mud Hens Baseball Club, Inc., rents the baseball facility from Lucas County at an annual rate of $1.00. In addition to Skeldon Stadium, the complex contains the Lucas County Fair grounds, the County Recreation Center, and the Ohio Baseball Hall of Fame. The Hall of Fame is a smaller version of the National Baseball Hall and features memorabilia honoring Major League Baseball players who are Ohio natives. The Ohio Hall holds inductions each fall during a Mud Hens game. There are 35 acres of free parking at the recreation complex; parking capacity is 21,000 vehicles.

Hens home games are broadcast via WFRO-AM and WMTR-FM radio. Listenership statistics and radio user demography have not been ascertained by the stations.

All International League teams are granted permission to originate radio broadcasts from Skeldon Stadium. The local cable system televises at least five Hens games per season using a four-camera set-up.

Price

The regular price per ticket to regular season Mud Hen's games is $5.00 for box seating, $4.00 for reserved seating, and $3.00 for general admission.

Children age 14 and under and senior citizens receive discounts of $1.00. Single-game tickets for designated special events, such as a Detroit Tigers exhibition game, and an annual "Toledo Tussle," an exhibition game featuring Tigers alumni, are $8.00, $7.00, and $3.00.

Season Tickets or Trade-In-Coupons

Mud Hens season tickets are called Trade-In-Coupons or TICs (Toledo Mud Hens Baseball Club, Inc., 1994g). Unlike traditional season tickets that entitle customers to attend each home game, TICs are redeemed for the games of their choice. TICs books contain 70 coupons, each worth one Mud Hens ticket. Holders of coupons have the option of calling to reserve their seat for any particular game or exchanging a coupon at the Hens' ticket office upon arrival. TICs books are available for box seating (guaranteed seating located within 50 feet of the playing field) at a rate of $210 or reserved seating (guaranteed seating located within 100 feet of the playing field) at a $180. rate. TICs books offer customers savings of nearly 50% off regularly priced tickets, and holders receive preferred parking passes. TICs are restricted for use at the Detroit Tigers Exhibition and Old Timers' games, Famous Chicken and Phillie Phanatic appearances, playoffs, and other special events games.

Mud Hens Trade-In-Coupons are sold by the Diamond Club, a group comprising baseball fans and other volunteers representing the civic, business, corporate, labor, and industrial leaders of Toledo. There are currently 100 Diamond Club members. For the past 16 years, the Diamond Club has sold over 1,000 TICs each season (Toledo Mud Hens Baseball Club, Inc., 1994f)

Diamond Club members are entitled to view Hens games from a modern skybox located behind home base. The skybox contains a food and beverage bar, lounge seating and tables, and enclosed box-seating. The Diamond Club box is also used for pregame parties for up to 30 guests. There are three methods by which interested persons may become Diamond Club members: (a) sell 15 season tickets (Trade-In-Coupon books), (b) purchase a radio advertising package for their businesses , or (c) purchase advertising and promotions packages amounting to $8,000.

Group Sales

Increases in group sales increases are a continuous marketing objective for the Hens, and some options are offered to attract groups and corporations to the games (Toledo Mud Hens Baseball Club, Inc., 1994d). Groups of 25 or more receive reduced-price tickets, same-location seating on pre-ferred sides (i.e., first, third, or home bases); entrance to Ned Skeldon Sta-dium two hours prior to game time; recognition on the message-score board; eligibility for Group Prize-Giveaways; box-seat tickets for future use for group's leader; and a special visit from Muddy. Groups of 100 or more may elect a group member to participate in a ceremonial first pitch. Group ticket sales are promoted through use of a brochure distributed at various high-traffic businesses (e. g., banks, restaurants, and gasoline stations) and by limited mailing (i. e., selected large and small businesses, industries, fans, and so forth). Pricing for group tickets is incremental depending on group size. Table 4 shows the rates for group and hospitality tickets.

Table 4
Rates for Toledo Mud Hens
Group Outings and Corporate Hospitality

Group Size	Box Seat	Reserved Seat	General Admission
25 - 99	$4.50	$3.50	$2.50
100 +	$4.00	$3.00	$2.00

Note. Adapted from *Toledo Mud Hens Group Outing Information*, p. 1, by Toledo Mud Hens Baseball Club Inc. Copyright 1994 by The Toledo Mud Hens Baseball Club, Inc. Adapted with permission of author.

The Mud Hens would like to increase reservations for certain types of group outings. The Mud Hens will work with customers to design individ-ually prescribed packages for special groups events. Events that have been popular in recent years that the Hens would like to stage for each home game are:

Pre-Game Picnics: The Mud Hens offer catered picnics, or "ballpark buffets," for any group. The picnics are targeted toward businesses, indus-tries, schools, families, sororities and fraternities, local or regional service groups, and so forth. The Mud Hens make picnics easy for groups by han-dling all arrangements for food and service. Muddy also visits and entertains at each picnic. There are two picnic areas in Skeldon Stadium: one located behind the extreme left field fence and another behind extreme right field.

Birthday Parties: The Mud Hens offer children's or adults' birthday cel-ebrations at Skeldon Stadium. All arrangements are made on an individual basis by the Mud Hens staff. Ticket pricing for adults' parties are off the rate card; food and beverage pricing is based on amounts and types of catering required. Pricing for children's birthday parties depends on the number of children and adults.

Corporate Hospitality: The Hens can accommodate corporation parties and outings (Toledo Mud Hens Baseball Club, Inc., 1994d). Group size is 25 minimum, but the Hens have cooperated on company parties of 2,000 guests. Ticket prices are determined with the regular group rate card, and amenities such as the first pitch, welcome message, and visit from Muddy and the players are offered.

There is no sales representative assigned specifically to groups acquisition, although an assistant general manager responsible for ticket operations handles all group requests not addressed by the Diamond Club. Groups order tickets by calling or faxing the Mud Hens box office. Payment is made by check, major credit card, or money order, and payment must be received by the Mud Hens no later than 2 days prior to game day. Tickets can be mailed to group leaders or may be obtained at the stadium. Rain checks for groups are provided in two ways: (a) groups may reschedule their outing, or (b) individuals may exchange their tickets for a future game. No refunds are available. Groups may receive special pricing considerations for all Mud Hens games except the Tigers Exhibition, Tigers Old Timers, Phillie Phanatic, Famous Chicken, and other such special-event games.

Summer Fun Packs

The Mud Hens offer two types of Summer Fun Packs to attract spectators to special events and the "bigger" Mud Hens games at Skeldon Stadium (Toledo Mud Hens Baseball, Inc., 1994b). Each Summer Fun Pack contains a different series of tickets. Table 5 shows the ticket contents of each Summer Fun pack.

Table 5
Contents of Mud Hens Summer Fun Packs

Summer Fun Pack # 1	Summer Fun Pack # 2
Mud Hens Opening Day (April 15)	Tigers Exhibition (May 9)
Tigers Exhibition Game (May 9)	Famous Chicken Night (June 9)
Famous Chicken Night (June 9)	Toledo Tussle (July 9)
Toledo Tussle (July 9)	Phillie Phanatic Night (August 13)
Phillie Phanatic Night (August 13)	Hall of Fame Game (August 19)

Note. Adapted from *Mud Hens Summer Fun Packs '94*, p. 1, by Toledo Mud Hens Baseball Club Inc. Copyright 1994 by The Toledo Mud Hens Baseball Club, Inc. Adapted with permission of author.

Summer Fun Packs cost $30.00 for box seats, $25.00 for reserved seating. Summer Fun Packs are marketed in the same way as group tickets (i.e., there is no specially assigned ticket agent, brochures are placed strategically throughout the region, sales are processed as received via phone or fax, and so forth).

Promotion

The Mud Hens promote their product through public service, community activism, and commercial means. A mix of public relations activities, paid advertising and commercial associations takes place throughout the calendar year.

Youth Camp

The Hens and a local sports medicine clinic sponsor a yearly Mud Hens Baseball Camp for girls and boys aged 8–13. The camp is held at Skeldon Stadium, and Mud Hens players and coaches teach fundamental skills. Enrollment is limited to 100 campers. Price of the 2-day camp is $50.00 (Toledo Mud Hens Baseball Club, Inc., 1994a).

Personalizing the Players

The Mud Hens organization collects feature-interest type information relative to Mud Hens players and uses it to help bring the players closer to fans and help player visibility within the community and media. Dossiers listing likes, dislikes, favorite movies, TV shows, vacations, and music preferences of players (and Muddy) are distributed to local media and are used by reporters in their news and feature stories about the Hens.

The management also encourages players to be active in the greater Toledo community by attending public service events; participating in pregame picnic appearances, autograph signings, children's contests and interviews, and making the rounds on morning radio and television shows.

Media Coverage and News Features

Toledo affiliates for ABC, CBS, and NBC television report Mud Hens scores and/or highlights on nightly sports newscasts, and each radio station in northwest Ohio and southeast Michigan reports Hens scores regularly on nightly or morning news broadcasts. It is not unusual for Toledo radio and television stations to report the Mud Hens scores ahead of major league scores, including those of the locally popular Tigers and Indians.

The fans' game-time activities (see section "Unique Features of Mud

Hens Baseball") are frequently reported in Toledo's major daily newspaper. Pictures of fans wearing their giveaway items on Martian Antennae Night or Funny Nose and Glasses Night or pictures of Muddy leading the bleacher section dance or rounding the bases in the children's baserunning contest appear prominently in either the sports or features section of the paper.

Frequent news releases are also prepared by the Hens media department. For instance, when the Hens return to Toledo after extended road trips, their return is announced by listing game dates, times, and the event of the game (such as a home run hitting contest for fans, Independence Day fireworks, Banner Day, and so forth).

Some celebrities playing in the Pro-Am Tournament associated with the LPGA Jamie Farr Toledo Classic have worn Mud Hens clothing during play. Professional basketball player Charles Barkley was the most recent Pro-Am player to be pictured in the daily newspaper wearing a Mud Hens cap.

Industrial Goods

Part of the Hens' plan to generate self-supporting revenue involves sale of advertising to local, regional, and national enterprise and numerous businesses use the Mud Hens' popularity to promote their own products and services (Toledo Baseball Club, Inc., 1994c). Signage is available on left- and right-field fences, scoreboard in center field, concourse, walkways into the stadium from the concourse, picnic and birthday party areas, and customer service desk. Rates for signs vary according to location and preparation. (Costs are increased if the Hens create and paint the signs.)

Prices for outfield signs range generally from $1,600 to $2,000 for a 10' by 14' sign or $3,200 to $4,000 for a 10' by 28' sign. Currently, there are 68 signs in the outfields. Concourse and walkway signs range in price from $600 to $800; there are four concourse signs and three walkway signs.

Advertising on the message center (Chad's scoreboard) is sold on a seasonal basis. Cost per season is $1,080 to show at least one commercial per game or $1,800 to show at least two per game.

Print advertising is also available in Hens' souvenir programs and scorecards. The *Ned Skeldon Stadium Souvenir Program* is 110 pages in length. Program ad costs are based on color, size, and/or location. Table 6 shows rates for program advertising. Costs of advertising are not subject to drastic increases from season to season. In fact, 1993 and 1994 advertising costs are identical. All program advertisers receive free general admission tickets for two special advertisers' nights held in June.

During each game, fans are invited to turn to specific ads in the program

Table 6
Rates for Toledo Mud Hens Souvenir Program Advertising

Back Cover	$2,500	Inside Front	$2,000	Inside Back	$2,000
Full Page	$2,000	Full Page*	$1,200		
Half Page	$1,750	Half Page*	$700		
Quarter Page*	$500	Eighth Page*	$300		

* Denotes black and white advertisement

Note. Adapted from *Toledo Mud Hens Baseball Club Advertising Rates*, p. 1, by Toledo Mud Hens Baseball Club Inc. Copyright 1994 by The Toledo Mud Hens Baseball Club, Inc. Adapted with permission of author.

to search for a lucky number. Special prizes are awarded to those fans who have the lucky numbers. Souvenir programs sell out each season. The Mud Hens' marketing department indicates that at least four other people besides the buyer read each program, and programs are saved for future value (Toledo Mud Hens Baseball Club, Inc., 1994c).

All scorecard ads are black and white; scorecards are contained in the Mud Hens program, which costs $2.00. Full-page score ads cost $1,200, half pages cost $700, and quarter pages cost $500.

Additional Advertising Opportunities for Sponsors

The Mud Hens also offer advertisers the opportunity to advertise on ticket backs, pocket schedules, special events postcards, and other mass distribution vehicles. Rates are negotiated independently.

Games are broadcast via WFRO-AM and WMTR-FM radio. Signals of both stations cover a critical radius encompassing all of northwest Ohio and southeast Michigan. Potential market size of these areas is 19 counties exceeding 3,000,000 persons (Toledo Mud Hens Baseball Club, Inc., 1994c). Giveaway merchandise and services are also awarded to listeners. Contests are conducted in ways similar to stadium contests except call-ins are required. Listeners win free cellular phones, weekend getaways, cash, free clothing, and so forth. Advertising space is available for pre- or postgame sponsorship, scoreboard shows, game MVP, and other. The Mud Hens also cooperate with advertisers by tailoring radio advertising programs specifically for their companies or services.

The Mud Hens offer various radio sponsorship packages to advertisers ranging from Flagship coverage (see Table 7; spots on all 144 Hens games broadcast on WMTR FM) to Network coverage (see Table 8; spots on all 144 games broadcast on WFRO-AM and WMTR-FM).

Table 7
1994 Mud Hens Radio Packages
and Costs for Flagship Coverage on WMTR-FM

Plan # 1 ($17,280)	Plan # 2 ($13,824)
Eight 30-second spots per game	Six 30-second spots per game
Opening & closing billboards	Opening and closing billboards
Twelve 30-second promo spots per week	Nine 30-second promo spots per week
2 season box-seat exchange tickets	2 season box-seat exchange tickets
Diamond Club membership	Diamond Club membership
Plan # 3 ($10,368)	**Plan # 4 ($5,760)**
Four 30-second spots per game	Two 30-second spots per game
Opening & closing billboards	Opening & closing billboards
Six 30-second promo spots per week	Three 30-second promo spots per week
1 season box-seat exchange ticket	1 season box-seat exchange ticket
Diamond Club membership	Diamond Club membership
Total costs per game: Plan #1 = $120 Plan #2 = $96 Plan #3 = $72 Plan #4 = $40	Total cost per spot: Plan #1 = $15 Plan #2 = $16 Plan #3 = $18 Plan #4 = $20

Note. Adapted from 1994 *Toledo Mud Hens Radio Packages*, p. 1, by Toledo Mud Hens Baseball Club Inc. Copyright 1994 by The Toledo Mud Hens Baseball Club, Inc. Adapted with permission of author.

Different packages apply for each type of coverage with costs ranging from $5,760 to $17,280 for 30-second commercials.

Advertisers can also purchase commercial time under three different contract rates for Mud Hens radio broadcasts. Table 9 shows the rates per season, month, or limited-time basis.

The Hens receive remuneration from the stations, but stations sell advertising and retain profits from advertising sales.

Table 8
1994 Mud Hens Radio Packages and Costs
for Network Coverage on WMTR-FM and WFRO-AM

Plan # 1 ($18,432)	Plan # 2 ($9,792)
Four 30-second spots per game	Two 30-second spots per game
Opening & closing billboards	Opening and closing billboards
2 season box-seat exchange tickets	1 season box-seat exchange tickets
Diamond Club membership	Diamond Club membership
Total costs per game: Plan #1 = $128 Plan #2 = $68	Total cost per spot: Plan #1 = $32 Plan #2 = $34

Note. Adapted from *1994 Toledo Mud Hens Radio Packages*, p. 1, by Toledo Mud Hens Baseball Club Inc. Copyright 1994 by The Toledo Mud Hens Baseball Club, Inc. Adapted with permission of author.

The Ballpark Is Open: The Hens WWW Page

The Mud Hens maintain a complete, updated World Wide Web page that reports both the latest and total-season game scores, records, and statistics (Toledo Mud Hens Baseball Club, Inc., 1997). Named "The Ballpark is Open," the page contains links that take Web visitors to the (a) Hens Press Box (for specific player information), (b) Mud Hens Store (to purchase souvenirs), (c) 24-hour access ticket office (with encryption for security), (d) Mud Hens Gallery (for a panorama of current and historic photographs), (e) business office (to answer FAQs), (f) Muddy's Buddies page (of special interest for children), (g) Hens library (for historical research), (h) Web Friends page (for Hens discussion groups), and (i) Hens mailroom (for interactive purposes and customer interface). The Hens page also provides linkages for TICs holders to use in making reservations. The Hens make advertising space available on each of the links.

Note: The preceding case as written deliberately contains some information that is directly related to marketing problem solving and some information that may be irrelevant and/or unrelated. Readers must glean appropriate data in order to successfully complete a case study; different types of information will be useful for different questions and/or solutions.

Table 9
1994 Mud Hens Costs for Advertising on WMTR-FM & WFRO-AM

Seasonal Spots	WMTR-FM		WMTR-FM & WFRO-AM	
	1 Spot	2 Spots	1 Spot	2 Spots
Half Season	$2,016	$3,744	$3,168	$5,760
Third of Season	$1,440	$2,688	$2,112	$4,032
Quarter Season	$1,080	$2,016	$1,584	$3,024
Monthly Spots	WMTR-FM		WMTR-FM & WFRO-AM	
	1 Spot	2 Spots	1 Spot	2 Spots
April	$690	$1,380	$1,012	$2,024
May	$900	$1,680	$1,320	$2,520
June	$840	$1,568	$1,232	$2,352
July	$900	$1,624	$1,276	$2,436
August/September	$990	$1,848	$1,452	$2,772
Individual Spots	1-50	51-100	Over 100	
WMTR-FM	$30	$28	$26	
WMTR-FM & WFRO-AM	$44	$42	$40	

Note. Adapted from *1994 Toledo Mud Hens Radio Packages*, p. 2, by Toledo Mud Hens Baseball Club Inc. Copyright 1994 by The Toledo Mud Hens Baseball Club, Inc. Adapted with permission of author.

Study Questions

1. What (who) are the Mud Hens' target markets relative to the primary marketing objective of maintaining attendance? What key elements in their current marketing strategy address the target markets?
2. Why do the Mud Hens continue to break attendance records? What makes the Hens unique in the Toledo market, and why do they retain their position?
3. As long as the Mud Hens continue to break yearly attendance records, will a lack of consumer demographic data have a substantial effect on the Mud Hens' marketing plan(s)? Why? What advantages would the

Hens gain if they had more complete data on their primary consumers (i.e., those who attend games)?

4. What elements of marketing should the Mud Hens consider in any research to maintain attendance status? What effects should the elements have on marketing strategy?

5. Identify those elements of Mud Hens games that may attract consumers (individual, group, family). What elements may be expanded, or what other elements may be developed to meet the attendance maintenance objective?

6. Which Toledo activities are direct competitors to the Mud Hens? Which are not? What data exist to show that events and activities of those types draw or do not draw similar consumers? Where are the data available? How should the Mud Hens deal with the competitors?

7. Identify some strategies and/or incentives that would help the Mud Hens meet their objective of more group ticket sales. How could Toledo's convention, travel, and tourism trade be accessed by the Hens?

8. Is it realistic for the Hens to expect that pre-game picnics, birthday parties, and corporate hospitality parties would be booked for each home game? Why? How could the Hens market those group sales more effectively?

9. With the success of the Diamond Club relative to season tickets sales (i.e., TICs), should the Hens continue to sell TICs through the Diamond Club? Why? What would be an advantage of hiring a TICs sales staff? Disadvantages?

10. What would be the Mud Hens' advantages of changing from TICs to traditional season tickets? Disadvantages?

11. Identify the strengths and weaknesses of the Mud Hens' per-game pricing structure. Should the Hens increase ticket prices? What does marketing literature indicate about price increases and their effects on consumption relative to sport commodities?

12. Do meaningful preliminary data exist to justify large expansion into secondary consumer markets (i.e., collectors or those with interest but who may not attend)? Should the Mud Hens take advantage of their national celebrity?

13. If they were to take advantage of their national celebrity, what types of marketing and promotion should the Mud Hens use in obtaining national consumer bases? What elements of their product line could be marketed nationally?

14. Would there be any advantage to making Hens' concessions products

(such as Mud Hens Pizza or Hens Ice Cream Sandwiches) available in local or regional stores? Any disadvantages? Should the Hens make the products available?

15. What ways can the Mud Hens justify their pricing of signage although lacking current demographic data? Should the Hens commit to defining their primary users? How should the Hens determine their fan base?

16. Design a demographic data collection for the Mud Hens that would reflect information from the entire season. Design the collection to be currently useful for a 7-year period (i.e., futuristic questions should be included; consider collecting data relative to information super-highways, computer ownership, access to Internet, and so forth, in addition to television, radio, newspaper usage).

17. Determine if the Mud Hens' radio/television broadcast arrangements with the local stations are satisfactory. If yes, explain why. If no, explain why, and outline a more suitable arrangement.

18. Formulate local and regional strategies to promote the Mud Hens and their product(s) during the off-season.

19. Suggest some additional promotional activities and giveaways for the Mud Hens.

20. Suggest some ways in which teams in the International League could cooperate in marketing strategies.

Suggested Readings

Bigelow, C. (1989, January). Spicing up your concessions profits. *Athletic Business*, 42.

Carolin, R. (1989, October). Involving local leaders generates community goodwill. *Athletic Business*, 24.

Ferguson, M. (1990, January). Reaping concessions profits. *Athletic Business*, 36.

Gordon, C. (1987, August). Taking a grassroots approach to research. *Marketing News*, 22.

Hofacre, S., & Burman, T.K. (1992). Industry segmentation theory and the sport industry: Developing a sport industry segmentation model. *Sport Marketing Quarterly*, *1*(1), 31–36.

Peppers, D., & Rogers, M. (1993). *The one to one future: Building relationships one customer at a time*. New York: Doubleday.

Pitts, B. G., Fielding, L. W., & Miller, L. K. (1994). Industry segmentation theory and the sport industry: Developing a sport industry segmentation model. *Sport Marketing Quarterly, 3*(1), 15–24.

Pitts, B. G., & Stotlar, D. K. (1996). *Fundamentals of sport marketing*. Morgantown, WV: Fitness Information Technology, Inc.

Stotlar, D. K., & Johnson, D. A. (1989, September). Stadium ads get a boost. *Athletic Business*, 49.

References

American League East: Top 10 prospects. (1994, February 7–20). *Baseball America*, p. 27.

Greater Toledo Convention and Visitors Bureau. (1994). *1994 official visitor's guide*. Toledo, OH.

International Baseball League. (1994). *International league record book 1994*. Dublin, OH.

O'Brian, R. (1993, March 15). Hen picked. *Sports Illustrated*, 78 (10), 10.

Reader survey results: Teams, dollars and sense, executive/non-player. (1994, January 10–23). *Baseball America*, p. 24.

Rousselot, C. (1992, January). No minor passion. *Future Stars*, pp. 22–23.

Toledo Mud Hens Baseball Club, Inc. (1994a). *Mud Hens and sports care present the Toledo Mud Hens 1994 Baseball Camp*. Maumee, OH: Author.

Toledo Mud Hens Baseball Club, Inc. (1994b). *Mud Hens summer fun packs '94*. Maumee, OH: Author.

Toledo Mud Hens Baseball Club, Inc. (1994c). *Toledo Mud Hens baseball: Every game's a big event*. Maumee, OH: Author.

Toledo Mud Hens Baseball Club, Inc. (1994d). *Toledo Mud Hens: group outing information*. Maumee, OH: Author.

Toledo Mud Hens Baseball Club, Inc. (1994e). *Toledo Mud Hens: History in the making* Maumee, OH: Author.

Toledo Mud Hens Baseball Club, Inc. (1994f). *Toledo Mud Hens 1994 media guide* Maumee, OH: Toledo Mud Hens Baseball Club, Inc.

Toledo Mud Hens Baseball Club, Inc. (1994g). *Toledo Mud Hens season ticket information*. Maumee, OH: Author.

Toledo Mud Hens Baseball Club, Inc. (1997). *The ballpark is open*. [Online] Available: World Wide Web http://www.mudhens.com/

Related Professional Associations

National Association of Professional Baseball Leagues
201 Bayshore Drive SE
St. Petersburg, FL 33701
Phone: 813-822-6937
Fax: 813-821-5819
Internet: http://www.minorleaguebaseball.com/info/about.html

Acknowledgment

The author gratefully acknowledges James G. Konecny, Assistant General Manager and Media Relations Director for the Toledo Mud Hens, for his valuable contributions to this project.

GENDER EQUITY ACHIEVED THROUGH STRATEGIC MARKETING

Richard L. Irwin, University of Memphis

● ●

Middle State University (MSU) was established in 1910 as a land-grant institution in the north central region of Minnesota. The university has a current enrollment of approximately 16,874 full-time students, 86% of whom are pursuing undergraduate degrees. Recently, the athletic program, which competes as a Division I independent, has encountered thorough scrutiny from the National American Collegiate Athletic Association (NACAA) for illegal activities by university alumnae. The review revealed that several overzealous alumni were providing male athletes with free use of automobiles and housing as well as cash payments with no services rendered. The 2-year investigation resulted in the football program's receiving a 3-year "Death Penalty" sentence as well as the firing of the athletic director, Howard Murphy, and the entire football coaching staff including two-time National Coach of the Year, Payton Fox.

Following an extensive national search, lasting over 6 months, Lu Ming was hired as the new athletic director for MSU. A former Olympic gymnast, Dr. Ming previously served as the Athletic Director at Eastern State University (ESU), an NACAA Division II school in New York City, for the past 5 years. Dr. Ming was considered a perfect candidate for the MSU position as a result of her accomplishments at ESU. During her tenure at ESU, the athletic department gained national acclaim for their gender equity achievements while maintaining a competitive position within the Northeast Athletic Conference (NAC). After inheriting an athletic program almost exclusively composed of males, Dr. Ming was able to balance participation rates that accurately reflected the composition of the university student body, which necessitated a 576% increase in females athletes' participation. Astonishingly, within the same time frame, participation among men increased 4% as well. Furthermore, Dr. Ming was able to secure over $1 million in athletic endowments to help support this valuable institutional mission while maintaining a competitive program.

Not everyone agreed with the hiring of Dr. Ming. There is a large group of male alumni who believe Dr. Ming is not the person for the job. Their contention is that MSU is a big-time athletic program in need of a big-time administrator. This group had a candidate of their own, Mr. Gerald "Jumbo"

Mitchell, a former MSU football star who has been serving as the assistant athletic director at the University of Central Minnesota for the past 3 years. Although Mr. Mitchell was interviewed for the position, it was the contention of the search committee that Dr. Ming not only possessed the skills necessary for "righting the ship" but was described as an "athletic marketing specialist," also a characteristic considered of great importance to the selection group.

Immediately following the hiring of Dr. Ming, Dr. Leonard Smith, an ardent supporter of the athletic department and close personal friend of Mr. Murphy, stepped down as university president citing personal health. Subsequently, Dr. Carol Davis, formerly President/CEO with BMI, a worldwide business machine corporation, was hired by the board of trustees to replace Dr. Smith. It was the opinion of the board that Dr. Davis, with a doctoral degree in marketing, possessed the requisite knowledge and skill to guide the institution into the 21st century. However, throughout the interview process and after the position was accepted, it was made abundantly clear to Dr. Davis that her first priority was to "clean up" the athletic department.

Adding salt to the existing wounds, within the first week of her presidency, an office aide provided Dr. Davis with an article from *US-Today*, a nationally popular daily news magazine, highlighting that MSU ranked at the bottom of all Division I intercollegiate athletic programs with regard to Title IX compliance. Unfortunately, Dr. Davis was not completely familiar with all of the issues related to Title IX. Although she knew the legislation had something to do with equal opportunities for males and females in educational programs, she was unsure how it related to athletics. As a result, she enlisted the help of Dr. Ming in addressing the situation. At the meeting, Dr. Ming provided Dr. Davis with several resources for enhancing her knowledge of the subject area. These included the actual Education Amendments Act of 1972, which included Title IX, Title IX Review Documents from the Office of Civil Rights, National Association for Girls and Women in Sport (NAGWS) Title IX Tool Box, and a variety of articles from *The NACAA News* on the topic of gender equity.

Dr. Ming indicated that the status of the MSU athletic program mirrored the situation she encountered at ESU, which eased Dr. Davis's mind considerably. Dr. Ming only had one request — that the President initiate the indicated actions. It was Dr. Ming's belief that a directive from the institutional CEO would command the attention of all athletic personnel. Dr. Davis was more than willing to fulfill this request after studying the provided materials.

Following the input from Dr. Ming and review of the materials, Dr. Davis called a mandatory meeting of all athletic personnel to deliver the following message: There will be no reinstatement of football, and within 3 years the athletic department WILL achieve complete equity with the following parameters:

1. Participation rates among male and female athletes as well as budgetary allocations accurately reflect gender-based enrollment rates which for the past 5-year period has been female dominated (48% male and 52% female);
2. There will be an equal number of men's and women's teams;
3. Current participation rates among male athletes must remain stable;
4. All promotional efforts aimed at attracting participants as well as spectators will be equitable as required under the provisions of Title IX; and,
5. All external funding opportunities such as sponsorships, booster donations, and endowments will be appropriated equitably among all athletic programs.

Without football, MSU will have 251 males participating in the following sports: soccer (32 athletes), wrestling (25 athletes), track and field (44 athletes), cross-country (28 athletes), baseball (35 athletes), basketball (14 athletes), hockey (27 athletes), lacrosse (24 athletes), and swimming (22 athletes). The women's athletic program has 115 athletes participating in field hockey (26 athletes), basketball (12 athletes), softball (16 athletes), track and field (23 athletes), cross country (15 athletes), and volleyball (12 athletes).

It now becomes the primary responsibility of all athletic department administrative personnel to develop an action plan that addresses the President's athletic equity mandate. Dr. Davis' only request is that the submitted plan follow a typical product-planning procedure, which, according to her, can be found in any fundamental marketing textbook and generally consists of (a) market research yielding product offerings, (b) product test marketing, (c) product modification, (d) production and product availability, (e) marketing mix manipulation, and (f) evaluation and feedback.

According to the President, it is imperative that the strategic plan address the following:

1. Recommendations for women's sports that are to be added to the MSU program complete with supportive rationale for inclusion;
2. Recommendations for the retention of all or some selected men's sports using an approach similar to the one described above;

3. Delineation of marketing strategies with supportive tactics that will be implemented for increasing as well as maintaining participation rates of both the male and female athletes at MSU. This should be done for each sport that is to be added/retained including information on the appropriate market growth vector to be employed (e.g., new market development) and the proposed marketing communications mix to be employed.

At this point the President has not indicated any budgetary limitations except for the fact that expenditures must be equitable. Therefore, possible acceptance of any plan appears to be based on the rationale with which it is presented.

Learning Exercise

In groups of four to five, develop a two-phase strategic plan as requested by Dr. Davis. For the purposes of this assignment, your plan need only consider equity relative to anticipated team participation rates. Be sure to construct strategy based on sound rationale.

Discussion Questions

1. Why is this a sport *marketing* case?
2. What should Dr. Ming's role be in this process? How should she delegate responsibility to her administrative and coaching staff?
3. How important is it that the President's background was in marketing?
4. Are there other groups or consumers in the community who will be affected by theses changes? Who? How?
5. What are some short-term consequences to be expected with this action? What are some long-term consequences to be expected? How should these be handled?

Suggested Readings

Branch, D., & Crow, R. B. (1994). Intercollegiate athletics: Back to the future? *Sport Marketing Quarterly, 3* (3), 13–21.

Carter, D. M. (1996). *Keeping score.* Grants Pass, OR: Oasis Press.

Frankel, E. (1992, November). Gender equity. *Athletic Management,* 15–19.

Mullin, B. J., Hardy, S., & Sutton, W. A. (1993). *Sport Marketing.* Champaign, IL: Human Kinetics Publishers.

NAGWS Tool Box. (1992). American Alliance for Health, Physical Education, Recreation, & Dance.

Sutton, W. A. (1987). Developing an initial marketing plan for intercollegiate athletic programs. *Journal of Sport Management, 1,* 146–158.

Professional Associations

National Association of Collegiate Directors of Athletics (NACDA)
P. O. Box 16428
Cleveland, OH 44126
(216)892-4000
http://www.nacda.com

National Association of Collegiate Marketers of Athletics (NACMA)
(440)892-4000, http://www.nacda.com/about/member/nacmomem.html

National Association for Girls and Women in Sport (NAGWS)
1900 Association Drive
Reston, VA 20191
(800)213-7193
http://www.aahperd.org/nagws/new-nagws.html

Women's Sports Foundation (WSF)
Eisenhower Park
East Meadow, NY 11554
(800)227-3988
http://www.lifetimetv.com/WoSport

Marketing a Basketball Tournament

Wayne Blann, Ithaca College

Background

During the early 1990s student-athletes of color at State University believed they were not being treated fairly with regard to selection and participation on varsity intercollegiate athletic teams, especially on the basketball teams. The student-athletes of color discussed this situation with members of the African-American and Latino Society (ALS) at one of the regularly scheduled meetings. The student-athletes of color expressed their view that the sports environment was hostile toward them and they were experiencing institutionalized ostracism. Because the student-athletes of color believed they were not being afforded fair opportunities to compete on intercollegiate sports teams, especially the basketball teams, they suggested that they wanted to work with the ALS to establish a basketball tournament for students of color.

In 1991 the State University African-American and Latino Society founded The Bringing Brothers Together Basketball Tournament. The purpose of the event was to offer a highly competitive basketball tournament for students of color (women and men) with a positive and supportive sports environment where the players' skills and talents would be appreciated and recognized by the community. During 1991–93, The Bringing Brothers Together Basketball Tournament was successful in developing competitive men's basketball games with a good number of participants/teams and some spectators. The women's basketball participants, however, were small in number, with few teams and few spectators. The participants and spectators comprised women and men of color who were students in the university. Because the ALS marketed the tournament only to students of color on campus, the event was limited in its scope and did not grow in size or popularity.

During 1991–93, the university's Educational Opportunity Program (EOP) Director, staff, and activities committee worked with The Bringing Brothers Together Basketball Tournament as a strategy for bringing EOP alumni back to the campus. The EOP Office made the basketball tournament the focal point of an EOP student and alumni weekend that included other activities to appeal to a larger and more diverse group of people. The EOP Office became a cosponsor with ALS of the newly named The Bringing

Brothers Together Basketball Weekend. The additional resources and leadership provided the ALS by the EOP office broadened the scope of the event, which was now marketed to all students, faculty, administration, staff, and EOP alumni. Those who participated and watched the basketball games were still primarily women and men of color, but some participants and spectators were white. The expanded market resulted in a larger number of men's basketball participants/teams with the games becoming highly competitive and very popular with the spectators. Likewise, the women's basketball participants/teams increased in number, became more popular, and were better attended. Other activities held in conjunction with the basketball tournament included a dinner/dance on Saturday night and a formal basketball awards banquet with a speaker on Sunday night.

Between 1991 and 1993, the event increased in size and popularity. However, between 1994 and 1996, the number of participants and spectators decreased with a significant decrease among women participants and spectators. In 1996 the men's basketball games were heavily marketed and somewhat successful, whereas little was done to market the women's games. There were so few women participants that it was not possible to organize games, so 3-on-3 basketball contests were held for women in place of the games.

Current Situation

In 1997 the university's Diversity Awareness Committee was consulting with the Office of Multiculturalism to identify ways to promote multicultural education and positive relationships among different groups of people in the university and the community. Representatives of the Diversity Awareness Committee and the Office of Multiculturalism met with representatives of the ALS and the EOP Office to discuss the possibility of reorganizing The Bringing Brothers Together Basketball Weekend to achieve these purposes. All groups agreed that changing the event so that it would promote positive relations among diverse groups of people and provide multicultural education programs was a worthwhile endeavor.

Developing a Marketing Plan

A task force composed of representatives of the ALS, EOP Office, Diversity Awareness Committee and Office of Multiculturalism was established to develop a proposal for The Bringing Brothers Together Weekend that would (a) clarify the mission, (b) establish clear objectives derived from the mission, and (c) identify programs/activities that could be marketed to specific targeted audiences to fulfill the objectives and mission.

The task force agreed that the basketball tournament would continue to be the focal point of the marketing strategy. It was further agreed that a special focus would be to increase women's involvement in the event, especially in light of gender-equity concerns currently being addressed by the athletic department. Finally, the task force agreed to consult with sport marketing experts (you and your classmates) to obtain their help in developing a marketing plan within the context of unifying the community and furthering social justice.

Questions for Study

1. Write a marketing mission statement.
2. Write specific marketing objectives derived from and linked to the marketing statement.
3. Describe specific marketing/promotions programs and activities that might be implemented to reach specific target audiences in carrying out the marketing objectives and achieving the marketing mission statement.

Suggested Reading

Blann, F. W. (1998). Sport marketing. In J. B. Parks, B. R. K. Zanger, & J. Quarterman (Eds.), *Contemporary sport management* (pp. 171–184). Champaign, IL: Human Kinetics.

Covey, S. R. (1989). *The seven habits of highly effective people.* New York, NY: Simon and Schuster.

DeSensi, J. T. (1994). Multiculturalism as an issue in sport management. *Journal of Sport Management, 8,* 63–74.

Grunig, J. E., & White, R. (1992). Communication, public relations and effective organizations. In J. E. Grunig (Ed.). *Excellence in public relations and communications management.* Hillsdale, NJ: Erlbaum.

Related Professional Associations

African-American Athletic Association

African-Latino Society, 953 Danby Road, Ithaca, NY 14850, (607)375-2538, http://www.ithaca.edu/admin/cca/cca2/als.html

Association of Black Women in Higher Education, c/o Nassau Community

College, Nassau Hall, Room 19, One Education Drive, Garden City, NY 11530-6793

Black Coaches Association, P. O. Box 4040, Culver City, CA 90231-4040, (888)667-3222, http://www.bca.org
Diversity awareness programs/offices on campuses
Minority affairs programs/offices on campuses

Colorado Xplosion of the American Basketball League

Dianna P. Gray, University of Northern Colorado

Introduction and Problem Statement

Lark Birdsong, General Manager of the Colorado Xplosion, and Anne Price, Director of Marketing for the Xplosion, were concerned about the problem of promoting the second-year franchise in a city that hosts five other professional sports teams. Given the success of the Women's National Basketball Association (WNBA) inaugural season, the task of positioning the Xplosion as a "major league" team in Denver was daunting. Even though the league office had done a great deal in getting the ABL off the ground, it was obvious to Birdsong and Price that the burden of promoting the team and attracting fans rested squarely on each franchise's shoulders.

Although Denver, with a metropolitan area population of approximately three million people, enthusiastically supports the Broncos (NFL), Rockies (MLB), and Avalanche (NHL), attendance at Nuggets (NBA) and Rapids (MSL) games has been spotty. Sold-out stadia are the norm for the Broncos and Rockies, and during the Avalanche's initial season in Denver, the winners of the 1996 Stanley Cup drew an average of 12,350 fans at McNichols Arena. McNichols, with a seating capacity of 14,500, is home for both the Nuggets and the Avalanche. The Nuggets, who struggled during the 1996 season and did not make the playoffs, were in the bottom third of the NBA in attendance figures for the 1995–96 season. The Colorado Rapids, a Major Soccer League franchise, had the lowest attendance figures in the league's inaugural year.

The ABL was established in 1995 to provide postcollegiate competition for elite female basketball players, build on the growing popularity of the women's college game, showcase the premier women's basketball players in the United States, and once the league began playing, take advantage of the tremendous success of the USA Women's Olympic team, winners of the gold medal in Atlanta in 1996. Colorado received one of the eight initial teams, making the Xplosion Denver's newest professional sports franchise. However, Birdsong and Price do not consider Denver's other professional sport teams as their primary competition. The University of Colorado's women's basketball team, perennially ranked among the top women's collegiate programs in the country, and the Women's National Basketball

Association (WNBA), the NBA-backed women's professional league that debuted in the summer of 1997, are direct competitors for a share of the women's basketball fan. In addition, Price sees the Xplosion competing with other entertainment options (attending movies, "malling," outdoor activities, etc.) for customers.

The American Basketball League

The American Basketball League (ABL) made its debut in the fall of 1996 with a 40-game regular season schedule and four playoff games. The league entered the market at a time when women's basketball was at its zenith in the United States, with the NCAA Women's Final Four selling out in advance for the fourth consecutive year and a gold-medal performance at the 1996 summer Olympic games still fresh in fans' minds. More than 13.5 million women play basketball regularly, nearly 25% more than in 1985.

In spite of the fact that the NBA-sponsored WNBA played to record crowds and enjoyed considerably greater attendance success than expected, ABL co-founder and VP Gary Cavalli believes that the ABL will be successful. Cavalli says, "We believe we have the right plan. We are just going to push forward" (Lister, 1996a, p. 3C). Table 1 profiles the eight teams competing during the ABL's inaugural season.

The Players for the First Season

Seven members of the U.S. Olympic team — Azzi, Edwards, Lacey, McCray, McGhee, Staley, and Steding — signed to play in the ABL. Unfortunately, not all of the Olympic team members chose to affiliate with the ABL. Some are playing in Europe or Asia, or chose to sign with the WNBA. Three of the most prominent Olympians — Lisa Leslie, Rebecca Lobo, and Sheryl Swoopes — opted to play with the WNBA. Although Cavalli would have liked to have signed all of the Olympic team's players, he is happy with the players who did commit to the ABL. "We actually got 80% of the people we wanted and a couple we hadn't anticipated" (Lister, 1996b, p. 3C). The average player's salary is $70,000; however, some players may earn as much as $250,000.

In an effort to generate more local and regional interest, the former Olympians and other marquee players were distributed among the eight franchises. Shelley Sheetz, an All-American at the University of Colorado, is just such a player for the Colorado Xplosion. Sheetz is joined by a number of other marquee players, including Charlotte Smith (Final Four MVP, All-American), Sylvia Crawley (1996 U.S. Olympic Team alternate, 1995

Table 1
American Basketball League Teams for the 1996 Inaugural Season

Team	Arena/Seating	Premier Player(s)	Coach
ATLANTA GLORY	Norcross (GA) 3,000 seats	Teresa Edwards (U of Georgia)	Trish Roberts
COLORADO XPLOSION	Denver Coliseum (16 games) 9,300 seats McNichols Arena (4 games) 14,500 seats	Edna Campbell (Texas) Sylvia Crawley, Charlotte Smith (North Carolina)	Sheryl Estes
COLUMBUS QUEST	Battelle Hall (OH) 6,700 seats	Nikki McCray, Carla McGhee (Tenn.)	Brian Agler
NEW ENGLAND BLIZZARD	Hartford Civic Center (Conn.) (8 games) 15,418 seats Springfield Civic Center (Mass) (12 games) 8,712 seats	Shanda Berry (Iowa)	Cliffa Foster
PORTLAND POWER	Memorial Coliseum 12,888 seats	Katy Steding (Stanford) Natalie Williams (UCLA)	Greg Bruce
RICHMOND RAGE	Richmond Coliseum (14 games) 11,992 seats Univ. of Richmond Robbins Center (6 games) 9,171 seats	Dawn Staley (U Virginia) Jackie Joyner-Kersee (UCLA)	Lisa Boyer
SAN JOSE LASERS	San Jose State Univ. Event Center 4,550 seats	Jennifer Azzi, Val Whiting (Stanford)	Jan Lowrey
SEATTLE REIGN	Mercer Arena 4,623 seats	Venus Lacey (Louisianna Tech) Cindy Brown (Long Beach State)	Jacquie Hullah

Source: *USA Today*, September 19, 1996, p. 3C.

USA Basketball Player of the Year), and Edna Campbell (1996 U.S. Olympic Team alternate, Pan-Am, & Jones Cup member).

The Competition:
The Women's National Basketball Association

The WNBA is the second new women's professional basketball league in the United States established during the 1990s. Unlike the ABL, the WNBA is a summer league and enjoys the support of its established parent, the National Basketball Association. The WNBA is also an eight-team league, all of the teams owned by the 29 NBA teams. During its first season, WNBA games were nationally telecast three times a week on NBC and cable channels ESPN and Lifetime, a first for any start-up league.

In addition to the backing of the NBA and a lucrative national television agreement, the WNBA signed some influential sponsors, including American Express, Coca-Cola, Bud Light, Champion, Nike, Sears, and Spalding. All have multiyear marketing partnerships with the league.

ABL Sponsors

Reebok, Lady Foot Locker, Nissan, First USA Bank, Phoenix Home Life Mutual Insurance, and Baden Sports Inc. are the ABL's national sponsors. Other companies are being courted, particularly in the women's athletic apparel category. During its first 2 years, the ABL negotiated about $10 million in league sponsorship agreements.

On the local level, businesses ranging from grocery stores and quick-serve restaurants to banks, hotels, and airlines are signing on as sponsors. In Colorado, *The Rocky Mountain News*, Norwest Bank, and Coors brewing have signed on with the Xplosion as local sponsors.

Table 2
ABL Profit/Loss Projections

Year	Projection
1996/97	$3 million loss
1997/98	$2 million loss
1998/99	$2 million profit

Source: *USA Today*, October 18, 1996, p. 2B

National Television

During the inaugural season of the ABL (1996), SportsChannel Regional Network televised 12 regular-season Sunday night games, as well as the ABL's All-Star Game, two playoff games, and the championship series.

The Xplosion appeared in three national broadcasts (Sunday night games) and five regional broadcasts (on Prime) as part of the national television package. For its second season (1997), the ABL signed a national television agreement with Fox Sports, and Nike has signed on to conduct a national advertising campaign highlighting various ABL players.

Marketing and Promotions

Xplosion Director of Marketing, Anne Price and her colleagues at the Xplosion are positioning the team as "superior entertainment value for the dollar" (A. Price, personal communication, October 8, 1996). There is a growing concern among sports fans that the major spectator sports leagues are pricing the product beyond the range of the average fan. Cognizant of this issue, yet not wanting to underprice and compromise the perceived value of the product, the Xplosion is offering a series of ticket packages and prices that will accommodate the majority of fans. Tables 3 and 4 list the season ticket packages and pricing chart for Xplosion games.

Table 3
Xplosion Season-Ticket Packages (per 20-Game Schedule)

Plan	Adult	Jr. (to 15) Sr. (60+)	Family (4 tickets)
Courtside A	$700	NA	NA
Courtside B	$400	NA	NA
Gold	$240	$220	$860
Silver	$200	$180	$700
Bronze	$160	$140	$540

Source: Colorado Xplosion 1996-1997 Ticket Information

In addition to the traditional marketing and advertising strategies (television, radio, outdoor, and print advertising), the Xplosion is conducting a grassroots promotional campaign. In an effort to introduce Denver to the ABL and the Xplosion, Birdsong, Price, and Xplosion players have been making a number of public appearances and accepting speaking engagements. In an effort to attract Denver's business community, the franchise has sponsored a weekly Hoops Cocktail Hour. Each week members of the business community are invited to the Xplosion's front office to meet the players and "talk hoops" with General Manager Birdsong and other front-office per-

Table 4
Xplosion Partial Season and Individual Game Ticket Information

Plan	Adult	Jr. (to 15) Sr. (60+)	Family (4 tickets)	Group (10+)	7-Game Price*	11-Game Price*
Courtside A	$36	NA	NA	NA	NA	NA
Courtside B	$21	NA	NA	NA	NA	NA
Gold	$13	$12	$47	$11	NA	NA
Silver	$11	$10	$39	$9	$74	$116
Bronze	$9	$8	$31	$7	$60	$94

Source: *Colorado Xplosion 1996-1997 Ticket Information*

* ABL Sampler partial season-ticket packages. The 7-game package exposes the ticket holder to every team in the league. The 11-game package is the equivalent to a half-season package. "Partial packages...the expense is small, the value extraordinary." (Colorado Xplosion 1996-1997 Ticket Information brochure).

sonnel. The initial response to the cocktail hour has been very positive.

Price is also working hard to get the public to know the Xplosion's players. Each week a different player is highlighted in *The Rocky Mountain News* (an Xplosion sponsor and print media partner) and the focus of game-day promotions.

Although it is well-known in professional sport circles that the foundation of a team's promotional program rests on close public relations work with all the news media in the region — television and radio stations, and newspapers — this is not as easy to achieve as it might appear. Given the number of professional and college teams in the Denver metropolitan area, competition for air time and print space is fierce. Additionally, the costs associated with a new franchise are enormous, and funds allotted for promotional purposes are limited. Birdsong and Price definitely have their work cut out in trying to market and promote the Colorado Xplosion.

Case Study Questions

1. Using information on situational analysis from chapter 4 of the Pitts and Stotlar (1996) text, analyze the Xplosion's situation in relation to its competitive, economic, and social environments.
2. What would you recommend Birdsong and Price do to market and promote the Colorado Xplosion for its second season of competition? Be specific in your sport marketing mix strategies (the four Ps).

3. At what stage are the ABL and, specifically, the Colorado Xplosion, on the sport product life cycle? What does this mean for promoting the ABL? the Xplosion?
4. How would you position the team? Justify your answer.
5. Do you think that the United States can support two women's professional basketball leagues? Be able to justify and defend your position.

Related Activities

1. Log onto the ABL's and WNBA's Internet sites, and evaluate how each league is promoting its teams on-line.
2. Compare the markets of ABL and WNBA teams. What does this tell you about each league's marketing strategies?
3. Contact an ABL and WNBA franchise and request a ticket-sales brochure from each. Compare how each league and team market and sell their product.
4. Conduct some focus group research with a group of 10 to 15 students on your campus to determine attitudes toward women's college basketball, the ABL, and the WNBA. Use your findings to help determine how you would market women's basketball.
5. Using your institution's library resources, determine the audience profiles for men's and women's basketball. Given this information, how would you segment consumers of women's basketball?
6. Develop an annual marketing plan for an ABL or a WNBA team. The development of a marketing plan for the upcoming season may help you to identify some of the emerging problems, opportunities, and threats associated with a relatively new sports league.

Related Readings

Carter, D. M. (1996). *Keeping score: An inside look at sports marketing.* Grants Pass, OR: The Oasis Press.

Cohen, W. A. (1995). *The marketing plan.* New York: John Wiley & Sons.

Colorado Xplosion 1996–1997 Ticket information brochure.

Horovitz, B. (1996, October 18). A basketball league of their own. *USA Today,* p. 1–2B.

Pearce, A. (1996, October 19). Women's team lives up to name. *Rocky Mountain News,* pp. 1C, 6C.

Pitts, B. G., & Stotlar, D. K. (1996). *Fundamentals of sport marketing.* Morgantown, WV: Fitness Information Technology, Inc.

Schaaf, P. (1995). *Sports marketing: It's not just a game anymore.* Amherst, NY: Prometheus Books.

Schlossberg, H. (1996). *Sports marketing.* Cambridge, MA: Blackwell Publishers, Inc.

Settle, R. B., & Alreck, P. L. (1986). *Why they buy: American consumers inside and out.* New York: John Wiley & Sons.

Stotlar, D. (1993). *Successful sport marketing.* Madison, WI: WCB Brown & Benchmark.

Suggested Trade Newsletters and Publications to Read

Advertising Age	*Brandweek*
Adweek	*Marketing News*
American Demographics	*Sports Business Daily*
Amusement Business	*Team Marketing Report*

References

Lister, V. (1996, September 19). ABL tries to court success. *USA Today,* p. 3C.

Lister, V. (1996, October 17). Pro game gets another go. *USA Today,* p. 3C.

FILLING YOUR FOOTBALL FACILITY WITH FANS — 17,000 OR BUST!

Dianna P. Gray, University of Northern Colorado

Introduction and Problem

Sitting in her office, Linda McLaughlin, the recently hired marketing director for Northern University Intercollegiate Athletics, and her assistant director, Mike Williams, contemplated their charge. McLaughlin had just been instructed by the Director of Intercollegiate Athletics to devise a plan to insure that attendance at home football games averaged 17,000 by 1999 and 20,000 fans per contest by the 2000 season. One of the primary reasons for setting this attendance goal was due to an NCAA requirement that Division I-A teams with a stadium capacity of greater than 30,000 average more than 17,000 in paid attendance per home football game at least one year in the immediate past 4-year period. Northern last fulfilled this attendance requirement in 1995 when they drew 86,685 fans in five home dates — an average of 17,337 fans per game. Because Northern failed to average greater than 17,000 fans per game for either the 1996 or 1997 seasons, the requirement must be fulfilled in one of the upcoming two seasons. As a first step to tackling this task, Linda asked Mike to gather information regarding the university, the Department of Intercollegiate Athletics, the Northern football program, and the environment in which the university operated.

Northern University

Northern University is a 4-year public institution located in northeastern Ohio in a town of 43,000. The University has an enrollment of approximately 23,000 students and offers nine different baccalaureate degrees in over 150 different career fields and 15 graduate degrees in 50 areas of study. Approximately 25% of the students reside on campus. Of those who commute, most live within a half hour to an hour drive of the main campus.

Northern University is located in the center of four major urban areas: Akron, Cleveland, Canton, and Youngstown. The University is easily accessible from these areas as well as a number of other major cities in Ohio and Pennsylvania. Its campus is attractive and nicely landscaped. The University recently celebrated its 87th anniversary as it was founded in 1910.

The Department of Intercollegiate Athletics

The Department of Intercollegiate Athletics at Northern University believes that its main purpose is "to plan and provide the best program possible for the students and community of Northern University." The department takes the position that it is but one part of the University and that it is committed to serving the institution. The department views its responsibility to foster and develop an atmosphere that allows the student-athlete to meet personal and professional goals, as well as career objectives.

Northern offers 20 Division I sports for its athletes — 11 for men and 9 for women. The Eagles are a member of the Mid-American Conference, a nine-school league that has produced champions in a variety of major sports. Northern University alumni include Jack Lambert, former All-Pro with the Pittsburgh Steelers and the late Thurman Munson, captain of the New York Yankees.

Facilities for the athletic program include Mix Stadium, an indoor fieldhouse and practice facility, ice arena, 18-hole golf course, all-weather outdoor track, and Memorial Gymnasium, which houses a 5,000-seat basketball and volleyball facility, gymnastics center, training rooms, and administrative offices. Mix Stadium is the largest in the Mid-American Conference, with seating for more than 30,000 fans. The stadium was constructed in 1969 as part of a $5.3 million bond program.

Northern University Football

The 1990s have not been easy for Northern University football. Most of the time Northern finds itself at the bottom of the standings in the MAC. In 1992, the Eagles went winless for the entire season and in 1993 and 1994 earned but one victory. In 1995, the team compiled a 4-7 win-loss record with a 3-6 record in the MAC. The combination of an intensive promotional campaign to increase attendance, including an extensive direct-mail campaign, Dallas Cowboy Cheerleaders half-time promotion at the homecoming game, and other attendance incentives, as well as improved on-the-field performance by the team, resulted in an increase in average home attendance to 17,337 (see Table 1). However, in 1996, absent a specific promotional campaign and a lack of further improvement in the team's win/loss record, average attendance figures again dropped to 7,014 fans per game, as the team posted a season record of 3 victories and 8 defeats. McLaughlin has reason to be encouraged, though, with the attendance figures for the 1997 season, with a 38% increase to a season average of 9,665. A combination of a greater emphasis on promoting the football team and a .500 season

Table 1
Football Attendance Breakdown by Year

Year	Avg. Student Attendance	Season Ticket Sales	Avg. Public Sales	Avg. Total Sales
1997	4,400	1,573	3,692	9,665
1996	3,381	1,441	2,192	7,014
1995	9,873	4,179	3,285	17,337
1994	2,725	1,848	5,717	10,290
1993	4,074	1,579	7,266	12,919
1992	6,556	665	2,437	9,658
1991	1,221	739	1,643	3,603

resulted in these improved attendance figures.

Competition for the Entertainment Dollar

The Northern football program has direct competition from a variety of small and medium collegiate athletic programs and other entertainment events in the Akron-Cleveland area. In addition, northeastern Ohio supports the Cleveland Indians and Cavaliers professional baseball and basketball teams, as well as a professional indoor soccer franchise, The Cleveland Crunch. Indirect competition from several other forms of entertainment, such as the Cleveland Orchestra, Cleveland Ballet, Rock-n-Roll Hall of Fame, and the flats (a popular, upscale revitalized area of Cleveland, which offers a variety of eateries and boutiques), among others, are factors that McLaughlin must also consider.

Ticket Information

At Northern, students with a valid ID card are admitted free to Eagle football games. This is possible because a portion of the general fee paid by all NU students is allocated to the Department of Intercollegiate Athletics.

Brochures regarding season-ticket packages are mailed in the spring to all previous season ticket holders, faculty and staff, Varsity N members, and Black & Gold club members. Season tickets are available at the cost of $60 for reserved seating and $85 for chairback seats (seats with a back between the 40-yard lines).

For the general public, general admission tickets are sold at the price of

$11.00 per game. Interested customers can obtain tickets in advance at the Northern ticket office, Memorial Gymnasium, via the telephone with a credit card, or at the stadium on the day of the game.

Demographic and Attendance Information

McLaughlin and Williams knew that they could not rely alone on a successful football season to attract fans. The football program, although working hard to try to get out of the MAC basement, probably would not be in the top of the conference standings, much less win the conference championship. However, both felt certain that given the success of previous promotional campaigns in increasing attendance, and the improvement in attendance figures for 1996 and 1997, achieving the attendance goal was possible in the next 2 years. Although the potential for increased season-ticket sales and increased attendance appeared to be attainable, McLaughlin realized that she needed more information before developing an appropriate marketing plan. After reviewing the demographic and statistical data currently available on the football program (see Tables 1 & 2), McLaughlin felt confident that there was potential for attendance growth at Northern's home football games.

Case Study Questions

1. Is Northern's football attendance problem unique? Why or why not? You should be able to support your answer with data.
2. What marketing mix strategies would you recommend to McLaughlin and Williams to help achieve not only the necessary average attendance figure of 17,000 but also a consistently near-capacity audience for future seasons?
3. What are the NCAA's regulations on football ticket sales promotions? How will these restrictions affect McLaughlin's ticket-pricing strategy(ies)?
4. What do the data Williams gathered tell you about the audience profile of Northern's fans? How can this information benefit McLaughlin as she develops a marketing strategy for the upcoming season(s)? What additional or different information would you include in the next audience analysis questionnaire?
5. What is a strategic analysis? Be specific in defining the components of a strategic analysis.
6. How can conducting a SWOT analysis assist McLaughlin and Williams in developing both short- and long-range marketing plans?

Table 2
Audience Profile of Northern University Football Attendees

Demographic	FB Season Ticket Holder	General Public	Students
Males	88%	90%	62%
Females	12%	10%	38%
White	78%	90%	72%
Black	22%	10%	28%
Married	83%	80%	NA
Single	17%	20%	NA
Average Age	49 years	38 years	19 years
Median Age	48 years	41 years	NA
Average Income	$39,571	$44,000	NA
Average Household Size	2.66	3.00	NA
College Educated	77%	40%	NA
NU Graduate	55%	20%	NA
Residence	NE Ohio	NE Ohio (Cleveland suburbs)	NA
Average yrs. Attending	9.4	4.1	NA
Attend with Friends	55%	40%	100%
Attend with Family	45%	60%	0%
Reason for Attending	Loyalty to NU	Like football Know a player	Know a player Fun
Like Most re: NU FB	Overall program	Excitement	NA
Like Least re: NU FB	Losing/No fans	Lack of fans	NA
Have Cable TV	77%	50%	37%
Listen To NU FB on Radio	77%	40%	20%

7. What marketing recommendations would you make to McLaughlin for the Northern football program? Be specific in terms of the relevant components of the marketing mix.

Related Activities

1. Find the NCAA News in your university library or the NCAA's home page on the World Wide Web. Periodically check for updated college football attendance figures. What are the trends regarding college football attendance?

2. Conduct some focus group research with a group of 10 to 15 students on your campus to determine their attitudes toward the university's football program. Use your findings to help determine how you might develop a promotional campaign that would attract more students to football games.

3. Work with the athletic department's director of marketing to develop an audience profile questionnaire and administer it at your institution (for any of the sports sponsored by the institution). Working in teams of three or four, analyze the data and prepare a written report for the Director of Marketing.

Related Readings

Carter, D. M. (1996). *Keeping score: An inside look at sports marketing.* Grants Pass, OR: The Oasis Press.

Gray, D. P. (1996). Sport marketing: A strategic approach. In B. L. Parkhouse (Ed.), *The management of sport: Its foundation and application* (2nd ed.) (pp. 251–289). St. Louis: Mosby.

Pitts, B. G., & Stotlar, D. K. (1996). *Fundamentals of sport marketing.* Morgantown, WV: Fitness Information Technology, Inc.

Schaaf, P. (1995). *Sports marketing: It's not just a game anymore.* Amherst, NY: Prometheus Books.

Schlossberg, H. (1996). *Sports marketing.* Cambridge, MA: Blackwell Publishers, Inc.

Settle, R. B., & Alreck, P. L. (1986). *Why they buy: American consumers inside and out.* New York: John Wiley & Sons.

Suggested Newsletters and Publications

Advertising Age	*Marketing News*
Adweek	*NCAA News*
American Demographics	*Sports Business Daily*
Amusement Business	*Sport Marketing Quarterly*
Brandweek	*Team Marketing Report*

SECTION 2

THE SPORT PRODUCTION INDUSTRY SEGMENT

The Sport Production Industry Segment: An Overview

There are many different products — goods, services, people, places, and ideas — needed to produce sports, recreation, leisure, or fitness activities. Some of these include facilities, equipment, clothing, shoes, officials, coaches, trainers, rulebooks, and governing associations. There are also many different products desired to influence performance in activity. Some of these include personal trainers, managers, fitness-enhancing equipment, performance-enhancing products, psychological training, first-class facilities and equipment, and specially designed clothing and shoes.

This segment of the sport industry contains those products needed or desired to produce a sports event or to produce or influence the level of performance of the participant. As such, some examples of products in this segment include sports equipment, sports facilities, sports officials, athletic trainers, and sports governing bodies. All of these are needed in order for a sports event to take place. Some of these are desired to influence the level of the event or the level of the athlete's performance. For example, we play softball with a softball, a softball glove, a softball bat, and softball shoes — equipment needed to play softball. We can possibly influence the level of our performance if we use a selected bat and glove and even cleats. Sport marketers of these products know that softball equipment will sell to those of us who want to participate in softball. They also know that there are some softball players who believe that their level of performance can be enhanced if they purchase and use specific equipment. Therefore, softball bats, for example, can range from a basic model with little promise of performance to a very expensive model with promises of enhanced performance — improved batting average, control, and distance.

Sport marketers need to know what the consumer wants the product to do in order to develop and design the product. The sport marketer can also use this information in promoting the product. Check your local newspaper for an advertisement for sporting goods or watch for commercials on television for a specific product. You can also go to a sporting goods store and look for in-store advertising, such as a sign next to the equipment. You will note that the ads speak to exactly what the consumer expects from the product.

The cases in this section include a variety of sport production products and involve several different marketing elements. In addition, the student will be challenged with ethical and professional issues relative to sport marketing.

Modern Turn for a Traditional Product: Cygnet Turf & Equipment

Jacquelyn Cuneen, Bowling Green State University

• •

Cygnet Turf & Equipment is a 5-year-old company owned and operated as the secondary pursuit of a successful physician who has an interest in farming and inventing. Douglas S. Hess, M. D., founded Cygnet because he could pursue his farming avocation and meet the demand for superior sod in commercial and residential landscape use. Cygnet began by growing a blue-grass product line and harvested the sod using the second most popular harvester machine in the industry. Cygnet also offered an added incentive to turf products buyers: Cygnet Turf would also install the sod (99.5% of sod farmers grow and deliver but do not install turf).

As business flourished, Hess found that a major problem in installing turf on large jobs is the ripping, tearing, and stretching damage that occurs due to tension when the sod is pulled during unrolling; pulling on heavy lengths of sod causes the sod to stretch and fit improperly. Also, forklifts were used to place the sod rolls; forklift placement proficiency is correlated to the proficiency of the forklift operator. If sod must be tugged into place because of an operator's misjudgment, seams, gaps, and weak spots result. To protect the sod from stretching and gapping, installers fixed mesh netting on the underside of the sod to protect it. After installation and settling, the netting tends to work its way up through the sod causing footing problems and injuries.

In 1988, Hess devised the plans for a sod-installation machine that would turn out sod without tearing or stretching it. Hess's blueprints re-sulted in several machines that are self-propelled with small engines, or re-quire use of small tractors to install large rolls of sod in a short time, yet do not harm the sod because the sod is merely being turned into place. Ma-chinery is calibrated so that rolls of sod (4 inches x 36 inches x 2 feet or 4 inches x 70 inches x 1 foot) are placed adjacent to each other with little or no manual adjustment. Cygnet Turf & Equipment holds U. S. and Canadian patents on the machinery; no other company in either of these countries may use the sod-installation machines.

The Sod and Turf Industry

Industry figures show that sales for nursery and greenhouse crops reached $8.4 billion in 1991, outselling wheat, cotton, tobacco, peanuts, sugar, and rice (American Sod Producers Association, 1993). The sod and landscape component of the farming industry caters to a niche market, yet Cygnet market research shows that there are 1,400 sod farms totaling 304, 200 acres in the United States. Typically, sod farms are 300 acres with most turf products distributed to landscape contractors in rolls or slabs. Cygnet Turf & Equipment grows, harvests, and installs only rolls. An American Sod Producers Association (1993) membership profile shows that the typical sod farm has been producing for 15 years; 67.8% are incorporated, 16.1% are owned by one person, and 16.1% are partnerships. Most sod farmers (57.5%) operate as cool-season growers (growing periods are interrupted due to harsh winters); 25.5% are transition growers (some interruptions occur) whereas 17.2% are warm-season growers (farms produce sod on a year-round basis).

Industry average shipping capacity is 25 tons carrying 1,080 yards of sod. Most growers deliver to sites between 31 and 75 miles of their growing sites (American Sod Producers Association, 1993). Table 1 shows the typical current market radius of sod growers, as well as the typical radius serviced 5 years ago.

Table 1
Typical Market Radius of Sod Growers

Miles Traveled for Delivery	% of Growers: 1988	% of Growers: 1993
1 - 30	21.7%	14.4%
31 - 75	40.2%	57.8%
76 Miles or Over	38.1%	27.7%

Note. Adapted from *ASPA Membership Profile Survey*, p. 2, by American Sod Producers Association. Copyright 1994 by ASPA. Adapted with permission of author.

Although just 80% of the acreage from a typical sod farm is allocated specifically for sod growth, 98% of the farm's income (increased from 95% in 1988) is traced to sod sales (American Sod Producers Association, 1993). Sales have increased slightly over the past 5 years (from 92 acres sold in 1988 to 100 acres sold in 1993). Industry median income for growers was $480,000 in 1992 against $443,150 in expenses. Industry average expenses were \$622,050; net worth of the average sod farm was \$1,929,667. Over one third (33.5%; Median percentage = 41.5%) of sod growers' budgets are used for salaries (average salary budget = \$153,000.).

Landscaping contractors have been the largest market for the sod industry over the past 5 years, but Cygnet Turf & Equipment has found a smaller niche market in sport facilities. Cygnet market research projects that artificial practice and playing surfaces for collegiate and professional football, baseball, softball, field hockey, soccer, and other outdoor sports will be replaced by natural turf surfaces as innovative forms of natural, durable sods are developed (Mazzeo, 1994).

Product

Cygnet grows, harvests, delivers, and installs large rolls of sod for sport, recreational, commercial, or residential use. Cygnet's primary product of sod is unique because of the technology developed to install it: The usual thickness of sod to be installed for sport, commercial, or residential use is slightly less than one inch. Cygnet's patented installation machinery enables sod rolls to be as thick as two inches and as wide as four feet. Thicker, larger rolls of sod are desirable for playing fields for several reasons, including (a) they are usable just days after installation; (b) they are more durable because of the thicker sod bed; and (c) fewer injuries occur because there are fewer seams, and the surfaces are more "fixed."

Cygnet technicians are able to grow specially ordered sod for use in certain climates or for special purposes. For instance, clients may have unique specifications such as (a) sod must be durable enough to withstand concerts, practices, and games; (b) it must have no excessively spongy or firm spots; (c) it must drain quickly; and (d) it must be able to withstand yearly extremes in weather and temperatures. Cygnet sod technicians will plant, test, and nurture different grass-types, then harvest, transport, and install the sod.

Cygnet Machinery: A Sole-Source Installer

Cygnet's overriding advantage in the sod product line is their proficiency at harvesting and installing larger rolls of sod. Cygnet farm-grown sod is installed by Cygnet's own technicians, who know the properties of the sod and have intricate knowledge of the patented sod-installation machinery; workers harvest, transport, and install sod with minimal damage to the product. Sod is harvested by lifting and rolling it into giant cylinder-type rolls (sod rolls are not unlike rolls of carpet in a warehouse). Rolls are transported to their destination, then removed and installed using Cygnet's patented installation machines. Because Cygnet's machines merely unroll the sod into place, workers do not pull and stretch the sod in order to create a good fit between pieces. Crews of four workers can install 4–5,000 yards (the equivalent of 1.5 football fields) of sod in one day using Cygnet's machinery, and fields are ready for use in a few days because of Cygnet's particular installation method (when Cygnet installed 15, 600 yards of new sod in Cleveland Municipal Stadium, the Browns practiced on the playing surface 5 days later).

Product Competition: Sod Installation

Cygnet market research shows six direct competitors for sod sales:

1. An Eastern-based company that also specializes large rolls. The company furnished the sod for a major league ballpark and an NCAA Division I-A football stadium, both located in the eastern United States. The company uses forklifts to place the rolls; forklift placing proficiency is correlated to the proficiency of the forklift operator. Seams, gaps, and weak spots result if the sod has to be tugged or pulled into place because the operator misjudged the placement.
2. A large, Midwestern multiservice farm (offering other greenhouse and nursery products) that installed sod in a newly constructed Midwestern Major League Baseball park. This company is more centrally located to Cygnet than to other competitors.
3. A sod grower in Cygnet's state that specializes in large roll bluegrass installations. This company has installed sod for a Major League Baseball stadium.
4. A sod grower in Cygnet's region that specializes in residential customers.
5. A small sod farm in an adjacent northern state, also specializing in residential and smaller commercial sites.
6. A sod grower in an adjacent northern state specializing in peat sod for sport installations. This company installed sod for an NCAA Division I-A football stadium.

Product Competition: Modern Installation Machinery

Cygnet market research identified just two North American competitors related to modern installation techniques:

1. A Midwest company that produces an installer comparable to one of Cygnet's. However, although Cygnet's installer permits rolls to turn

out sod smoothly, this company's installer is designed in such a way that workers must pull the rolls in order for them to unwind. Mesh netting must be attached on the underside of the sod to protect the sod from tearing. The company is very visible in the marketplace because it advertises heavily on the national level.

2. A southern-based company that produces an installer model comparable to one of Cygnet's. Like the machine used by Cygnet's in-state competitor, this company's installer is designed so that sod must be pulled from rolls. The southern-based company does not advertise extensively on national levels.

Forms of Cygnet equipment are being used currently in the United Kingdom. Cygnet Turf & Equipment is investigating the feasibility of producing and manufacturing their patented equipment for retail sale in North America.

Place

Cygnet Turf & Equipment is located in Cygnet and North Baltimore, Ohio, small communities located approximately 40–50 miles south of Toledo on Interstate 75. Cygnet plants 150 acres of land; 100% of land production is devoted to developing and perfecting sod. Cygnet has expansion capacity to 1,500 acres.

Sod products are shipped to sites via interstate highway from North Baltimore using flatbed trucks contracted by Cygnet. Cygnet is in constant touch with drivers and technicians at the site to monitor and time deliveries. Deliveries arrive at the site every hour and 10 minutes. Using this "pipeline" system, machinery handles sod rolls just once when sod is removed directly from the flatbed and placed on the installation machine. Many Cygnet competitors deliver entire orders of sod in one trip; machinery removes the sod from the truck, stores it in advantageous places on the ground; then machinery lifts the sod again when it is time for placement. Cygnet's system is "kinder" to the product. Consistent with industry averages, most of Cygnet's sod products are sold to landscape contractors. Table 2 shows the industry averages for types of sod sales.

Currently, Cygnet's main distribution relative to sport markets is primarily regional. Cleveland Municipal Stadium (prior to its destruction), the University of Michigan, The Ohio State University, the University of Findlay, and Defiance College all have Cygnet-grown and -installed sod in their stadia. However, Cygnet has the resources to deliver and install their products anywhere in the United States and was the major grower and installer

Table 2
Sod and Turf Product Customers for 1988 and 1993

Customer	1988	1993
Landscape Contractors	44.6%	40.0%
Homeowners	15.0%	14.0%
Nurseries or Garden Centers	7.9%	12.0%
Builders	12.0%	9.0%
Golf Courses	4.7%	8.0%

Note. Adapted from *ASPA Membership Profile Survey*, p. 3, by American Sod Producers Association. Copyright 1994 by ASPA. Adapted with permission of author.

for the sod in Miami's Joe Robbie Stadium (NFL Dolphins). Distribution is arranged by contract and dependent on order size and distance traveled. Average truck capacity for the industry is 25 tons; average load transported is 1,080 yards of sod (American Sod producers Association, 1993). Cygnet figures are consistent with industry averages.

When customers wish to purchase sod products from other sod vendors, they may contract with Cygnet to install the sod with their patented installation system. Trucking is arranged by Cygnet, and the pipeline delivery method is used. This accounts for a small portion of Cygnet's business; most contracts call for Cygnet to both supply and install sod.

Promotion

Industry average advertising expenses were $15,029 (median = $6,125; 1.6% of total operating budgets). Table 3 shows the typical advertising venues for the turf industry.

Cygnet figures show that their advertising and promotion expenditures exceed industry averages. Currently, Cygnet's sole promotional strategy involves advertising in various trade journals and participating in turf industry and related trade shows.

Cygnet has relied heavily on word-of-mouth promotion. Cygnet has earned an exemplary reputation among sod customers and has obtained many contracts due to satisfied customers. Many sod growers and installers have had to replace or reinstall their products due to substandard products or insufficient installation; no Cygnet job has had to be redone due to faulty growing or installation methods.

Table 3
Typical Promotional Media Used by Sod Growers

Media	1988	1993
Customer Referral	82.0%	86.0%
Yellow Pages	79.5%	86.0%
Direct Mail	42.5%	44.2%
Newspaper	35.0%	41.9%
Trade Shows	35.0%	39.5%
Trade Journals	20.0%	33.7%
Radio	10.0%	14.0%

Note. Adapted from *ASPA Membership Profile Survey*, p. 2, by American Sod Producers Association. Copyright 1994 by ASPA. Adapted with permission of author.

Immediate Promotional Plans

In 1994, Cygnet obtained the services of Mary Beth Mazzeo, an independent marketing researcher, who proposed a marketing plan for the company (Mazzeo, 1994). She identified several immediate needs for promotional success:

1. Cygnet should use a standard logo in all promotional efforts. The logo created shows a cygnet swan outlined in a solid oval with the company name integrated prominently with the artwork.
2. A stationery system (logo letterhead, envelopes, etc.) should be created and used for all company correspondence.
3. Uniform business cards using the logo should be designed for each company representative.
4. A professionally produced videotape showing Cygnet's harvesting and installation procedures should be prepared and sent to inquiring customers.
5. Succinct brochures and other promotional materials should be prepared.
6. Direct mail advertising should be used four times per year for smaller clients and more frequently for larger accounts.
7. Cooperative arrangements should be made with multiproducts nursery and garden retailers. Cygnet literature should be available to a "do-it-yourself" market, as well as large sport and commercial markets.
8. Databases should be established in order for Cygnet to conduct large

business on an individualized level. Databanks will help Cygnet market on a personalized level.

9. A newsletter should be published quarterly in order to maintain contact with customers. The newsletter that was created ("Cygnet Sod Turf Times") contains information about Cygnet's latest inventions, grass recycling, sodding, and a question and answer column.

10. Cygnet should increase their associations with industry trade shows.

11. Camera-ready artwork should be created, and preproduction print should be completed by Cygnet in order to offset advertising costs.

12. Specialty advertising items (novelties, pens, pencils, notepads, and so forth) using Cygnet's logo should be created and distributed at trade shows and with each inquiry.

13. Cygnet's print advertising should be of display rather than classified type. Print advertising should be placed in U. S. and Canadian markets.

14. Radio should be used as an advertising medium in spring and summer. Cable TV should also be used as an advertising medium.

15. Media lists should be compiled and retained, and records of ads and expenditures should be analyzed regularly.

Strategic Objectives

Cygnet's management and marketing executives have identified several short- or long-term goals (Mazzeo, 1994) related to market penetration (new users of new products) or market development (reselling newly developed or additional products to current customers):

1. Build and sell the best machinery on the market (long term).
2. Sell 70 acres of sod locally (short term).
3. Complete four major installations (short term).
4. Sell ten 30-inch layers of sod in inventory currently (short term).
5. Complete negotiations with an engineering firm to build and install machines domestically (short term).
6. Build a loyal customer base (short and long term).
7. Develop a solid promotional plan (short term).
8. Develop a system of dealerships for 30-inch machines (long term).

Price

Price of sod rolls varies according to types and amounts of sod and dimensions of grounds. Price for Cygnet machinery installation varies as a function of the same variables. Residential and landscape contractor accounts comprised 96.9% of Cygnet's business in 1993. Sport field sales and installation contracts accounted for 3.1% of business, yet Cygnet's income statement translations showed that these contracts accounted for one quarter of 1993 cash receipts. Large-roll installation accounted for most overall receipts in 1993 (54.3%), with 31.2% of income derived from machine sales, and 4.1% from small-roll sales (Mazzeo, 1994).

Industry averages indicate that 85% of sales are to wholesale markets with 15% to retail sales. Cygnet's sod prices do not vary according to wholesale or retail trade: All buyers pay the same price for sod products. Cygnet has no records to show if wholesale buyers of their products increase prices in resale on the retail market.

Note: The preceding case as written deliberately contains some information that is directly related to marketing problem solving and some information that may be irrelevant and/or unrelated. Readers must glean appropriate data in order to successfully complete a case study; different types of information will be useful for different questions and/or solutions.

Questions for Study

1. The average market radius for the turf growers has decreased relative to longer distance jobs over a 5-year period, and increased for some shorter distance contract sites (see Table 1). What effect will this have on the turf industry? What measures could turf growers and sellers take if their farms are longer distances from the larger jobs available?

2. Cygnet's larger jobs relative to sport complexes have been completed at various distances from North Baltimore (from a half hour away to 48 hours away). Does Cygnet need to be concerned about market trends relative to distance? What factors should Cygnet consider in assessing the distance trends?

3. What are Cygnet's prospects for gaining an entire North American rather than regional market? What factors should Cygnet consider in international promotions?

4. Cygnet is unique due to its sole-source installation status. Describe the benefits of being a sole source for installation. Should Cygnet concentrate on installations exclusively? What benefits would Cygnet have if they were exclusively an installation company ?

5. How will Cygnet be affected if other growers decide to install as well as grow sod? What ramifications will Cygnet feel if other growers use

Cygnet's machinery to install sod? Will Cygnet's long-term goal relating to manufacturing equipment affect their market advantage? How should Cygnet distribute sod-installation machinery without depleting their own markets?

6. What factors should Cygnet consider in identifying their primary markets? Should Cygnet abandon the residential and commercial market and concentrate on the sport and recreational market? Should their decision be based on job type? That is, what factors should Cygnet consider in maintaining a local residential and commercial sales base, but a national sport and recreation sales base?

7. Market trends for the turf industry show that sales to typical buyers have declined slightly over the past 5 years (see Table 2), yet Cygnet's frequency of sales has increased relative to commercial, residential, and sport facility customers. What factors have contributed to Cygnet's atypical growth during a declining period for the turf industry?

8. Analyze Cygnet's competition base. Does Cygnet's competition base merely relate to growing? Does Cygnet have any genuine current competition for installation?

9. What are the trends in outdoor sport and recreational facility construction relative to playing surfaces? Are newer stadia and parks installing artificial or natural turf? What factors are considered in field construction? What are the construction trends in stadium and park renovation?

10. Devise plans that will enable Cygnet to meet its strategic marketing goals in the short and long term.

Suggested Readings

Graham, J. R. (1994, January/February). Marketing turfgrass sod: Use value added to increase business. *ASPA Turf News*, pp. 14–15.

Peppers, D., & Rogers, M.. (1993). *The one to one future: Building relationships one customer at a time*. New York: Doubleday.

Pitts, B. G., & Stotlar, D. K. (1996). *Fundamentals of sport marketing*. Morgantown, WV: Fitness Information technology, Inc.

Surviving the storm: Dealing with price wars, competition and the economy. (1993, September/October). *ASPA Turf News*, pp. 52–58.

Wildmon, J. (1993, May). Turfgrass renovation: Measures for success. *Sports Turf*, 14–17.

References

American Sod Producers Association. (1993, November/December). *1993 ASPA membership profile survey*. Author.

Mazzeo, M. B. (1994). *Cygnet Turf & Equipment: Strategies of success*. Cygnet, OH: Cygnet Turf & Equipment.

Related Professional Associations

Turfgrass Producers International (TPI)

1855-A Hicks Road

Rolling Meadows, IL 60008

Phone: 708-705-9898

Fax: 708-705-8347

Note. Effective July 24, 1994, the American Sod Producers Association (ASPA) membership voted to change the name of the organization to Turfgrass Producers International.

Acknowledgments

The author gratefully acknowledges Mary Beth Mazzeo, Marketing Consultant, and Richard Mazzeo, Business Manager for Cygnet Turf & Equipment, for their valuable contributions to this project.

NORTHERN LIGHTS, INC.

David Stotlar, Northern Colorado University

Directions

As the marketing team for Northern Lights, Inc. (NLI), this case will help you become aware of the challenges facing the start-up of a new company and in developing a respectable presence in several market areas. Careful monitoring of market conditions, evaluation of market needs, rapid response to market requests, and adjustment of marketing techniques must all be recognized as mandatory and included in market planning and research. These are all predicated on high-quality market research.

You are a member of a four-person marketing team that is in place and functioning full time. Initial product development is in the final stage with units scheduled for release during the first quarter of the coming year. Marketing goals, definition of strategies, selling activities, and budgets are all being completed. Extensive business and financial planning activities have been completed. Your task is to complete the market research for implementation of the marketing plan.

Introduction

Northern Lights, Inc. (NLI) has recently been incorporated under the laws of the State of Colorado as an applied technology company specializing in the development, manufacturing, and marketing of lighting products for sport utility vehicles (Jeeps, Blazers, Explorers, etc.). The overall company management, including marketing activities, is handled by Mr. Juan Hernandez, President and Chief Executive Officer, who has over 22 years' management and sales experience. Product design, purchasing, production, and quality control are managed by Ms. Althea Hayward, Vice President of Engineering and designer of NLI products. She is the owner of seven patents on various mechanical and electromechanical devices.

The immediate goals of the company include (a) short-term capitalization, (b) initial product introduction, (c) product sales, and (d) breaking even within the first year's operation. Guidelines for product development indicate that the product concepts must be market driven in an identifiable market. Long term goals include (a) expansion of the product lines, (b) expanded distribution, (c) research and development of new products, and (d) custom product development through a subsidiary division.

None of the NLI's products are presently being marketed; however, the initial product has been developed and can be seen in Figure 1. Manufacturing cost estimates indicate that the primary auxiliary lighting system can be priced to sell in the $50 range. Market surveys also verify the price as acceptable. At this level, NLI will have a strong initial net profit margin of $25 per unit over the first 100,000 units. All sales over this figure generate a profit of $35 per unit. Projected sales must quickly establish a healthy cash position to aid in absorbing the necessarily higher marketing costs accrued during the start-up period. In the succeeding year, reductions in costs resulting from improvements in manufacturing processes and possibly better component purchases are projected to increase profit margins by 10%.

The North Star

High-Power 130 & 100 Watt
Quartz-Halogen Auxiliary Lights

LOW PROFILE

Figure 1

To determine the feasibility and marketability of the NLI line of products, many demonstrations were conducted during the development period to assess consumer interest. Particular attention was paid to comments regarding consumer acceptability and changes were instituted to improve operation and/or design. Included in the market survey was participation in last year's Specialty Equipment Market Association (SEMA/AI) show held in Las Vegas, Nevada, which attracted 29,672 domestic buyers and 6,643 from international markets. SEMA is a support organization for the majority of the after-market automotive manufacturers and suppliers. Comments from this show were most favorable, and contacts with many potential wholesale and catalog suppliers were established.

The trade show and general market research indicate that the typical user benefits of auxiliary lighting systems fall into three categories: functional, economical, and psychological. More specifically these comprise

Functional

1. The mounting framework provides a secure location for the lighting system without defacing the vehicle.
2. A lighting system is an auxiliary device that enhances the vehicle's

factory-installed lighting and road illumination.

3. The interchangeable colored lenses permit expanded marketability — that is, red/red for firefighters, red/blue/clear for law enforcement, and amber/amber for construction and public utility vehicles.

Economical

1. According to the *NADA Official Used Car Guide*, auxiliary lighting enhances the resale value of sport utility vehicles approximately $125.00 at wholesale and $150.00 on the retail market.
2. If used for business purposes, that is, volunteer fire use, construction, or law enforcement, the unit may be deductible as a business expense and the cost added to the value of the vehicle and included in the depreciation of that vehicle.
3. The units can be removed from the vehicle being sold or traded and reinstalled on a replacement vehicle with only minor effort.

Psychological

1. Confidence of superior visibility leads to added safety.
2. Feeling of being contemporary; "having the latest gadget." (Market studies indicate that 14% of Americans want to be first in line for a new product.)
3. Satisfaction of having increased the value of the vehicle.
4. Satisfaction of minimizing income taxes if (purchase price is tax deductible and unit can be depreciated with vehicle), in accordance with federal tax laws.

NLI intends to operate as a customer-oriented company and build a favorable industry reputation. The company offers and honors a one-year limited warranty against defects in workmanship and material. Financial projections include a warranty expense generated by the outright replacement of .5% of all units sold at retail costs. Defective units will be held with no repair action taken. Information obtained from units returned will be monitored, and as indicated, design or production changes will be considered. The establishment of a system for repair of defective units will be considered when indicated by economics. The cycle of market development and sales activities is consistent with historical norms for successful introduction of vehicular lighting systems.

NLI may wish to increase marketing activities across the broad potential market base of long-term and fleet users. This might be accomplished by expanding the refined direct selling approaches into additional segments within the broad market as well as wholesale distributions through established mail order and mass merchandising outlets. Fleet markets are considered long term because of the amount of official red tape involved in establishing product acceptance by municipalities purchasing from fleet operations.

The company has retained financial and business planning counsel from Bankers International Corporation, which is an experienced business planning and development firm, in order to be poised for an initial public offering (IPO) when it is most beneficial to the company and its stockholders. Your management team must carefully consider the areas in which strength is required to successfully compete and develop beyond the initial product introduction. The company has selected financial, legal, and business planning counsel capable of serving as an integral part of the management team throughout the planned growth.

Financial projections indicate that NLI should quickly become a cash-strong company. It is recognized, however, that the company may wish to expand its marketing and new product releases more rapidly than can be supported by sales alone. NLI may, therefore, strive to position the company as an attractive candidate for an IPO during the first years of operation. This option may be exercised as a function of the IPO market and the company's expansion needs to meet market demands or competition. Management is also developing strategies that will position the company as an attractive candidate for acquisition or merger on the strength of its market position.

Question: What financial and legal decisions in the interim should be made with the IPO option in mind?

Initially NLI will purchase its inventory requirements in the United States to maximize its control of all facets of manufacturing and marketing. The company, to ensure its competitive edge, may actively pursue alternate component and subassembly sources including possible overseas suppliers. Preliminary discussions are presently in process with several overseas importers and liaison firms. The results of this investigation provide valuable input for any planned NLI expansion into international markets.

The ability to compete successfully in the long term is based on the company's continued efforts in thorough planning, attention to customer needs, product quality, realistic assessments of marketing challenges, and updating and implementation of stated goals.

Question: What profit is needed to generate a positive cash flow through product sales within the first year following the national introduction of the initial product?

Question: What percent of the available market will be needed to achieve this goal?

Question: Which market strategies or techniques need to be implemented during the year to achieve these goals?

Marketing Environment

Last year, aftermarket sales of sport utility vehicle off-road and recreational lighting systems were, according to published figures, in excess of $894,000,000. This rather sizable amount covers a broad market of recreational and off-road equipment purchasers and includes specific and targetable submarket groups, such as volunteer firefighters, construction companies, public and private security companies, and law enforcement entities. Additional market extensions include government and military users. There are in excess of 30 domestic manufacturers of aftermarket vehicular lighting devices. Twenty of the manufacturers are classified as large corporations and account for 88% of the business generated. The general market for aftermarket vehicle lighting has been growing at a rate of about 15% per year.

Question: In the domestic market, approximately how many vehicles are currently equipped with some type of auxiliary lighting device?

Question: What does your research indicate as a market size for additional, unique lighting products in previously untapped or inadequately supplied markets?

Company research indicates that the international potential for NLI products appears to be considerably larger than that of the domestic market.

Question: Do your data support this finding?

Question: What steps should be taken to secure foreign patents and to develop long-range plans to penetrate those markets?

Immediate goals, objectives, and activities for your marketing team include:

- Generate a positive cash flow through product sales by the seventh month following the national introduction of the initial product.
- Penetrate one and one-half percent (1 1/2%) of the available market for the entire product line by the end of 3 years.
- Define market strategies (media uses, direct mail programs, and tradeshow selection) or the wholesale marketing techniques, or both, to beimplemented during the coming year.
- Complete the agreements necessary to implement product sales through at least one nationwide distributorship catering to sport utility vehicle auxiliary lighting products.
- Complete offshore production analysis and locate potential sources for subcontract or joint venture production.

Long-term objectives for your marketing team include:

- Enhance product-line development and implement revised and tested marketing strategies.
- Expand and refine product marketing with the addition of wholesale outlets.
- Solidify marketing arrangements with mail order and catalog firms initially contacted. The goal is to have catalog advertising circulating to five million household and/or consumer outlets within 5 years.
- Complete marketing arrangements with at least five fleet operations with combined sales of 100 or more vehicles.
- Position NLI as an attractive candidate for an IPO initial public offering, merger, or   acquisition during the next 3 years.
- Positioning NLI, through continued expansion nationally and internationally, as a leading supplier for the aftermarket demands for sport utility vehicle lighting products.

Market Size and Identity

Question: How many people in the United States own and use sport utility vehicles in some type of recreational or business activity?

Some business activities require the use of some sort of vehicle-mounted safety or emergency lighting device as well as sport and recreational use. In addition to the primary target market identified above, there may be discreet and targetable submarket groups, such as fire departments with both municipal fire-fighting professionals and volunteer firefighters. Construction companies and private security companies also utilize similar vehicles and trucks, many of which could be equipped with your products.

Question: What data is necessary to project market size based on the primary and secondary markets you select?

Market Characteristics

General trade journal reports indicate that a substantial portion of the personal market for these lighting systems comprises individuals characterized as "affluent" consumers (households with incomes greater than $75,000 in 1998), who have been the subject of extensive studies regarding attitudes and buying habits. This affluent market is growing at 8.6% per year in the 1990s. These studies have found that this market's primary purchase motivators are convenience and quality.

Question: Can you present data that either support or refute these general findings?

NLI may wish to increase marketing activities across the broad potential market base of long-term and fleet users. These markets include sales for private and public utilities trucks, forestry and lumber trucks, military and border patrol/immigration vehicles, municipal and volunteer fire equipment, and the large number of law enforcement vehicles throughout the United States.

Question: Should NLI increase its market activities across the broad potential base by expanding the refined direct selling approaches, by increasing the number of wholesale distributors, and by adding mail order and mass merchandising outlets?

Custom-Design Markets

Through a subsidiary corporation, NLI has the ability to custom design vehicular lighting systems for entire police forces, fire and rescue, highway patrol, security patrol, municipal fire departments, and any other group utilizing vehicular lighting systems similar to existing products. Custom-designed products for this market, developed in the future, are expected to be highly profitable additions to the current product.

Question: When would be the best timing for initiation of these activities?

The marketing environment consists of 30 domestic manufacturers of aftermarket vehicular lighting devices with the top 20 accounting for 88% of the market. To analyze each of the competitive manufacturers is cost prohibitive. Therefore, analysis of the competition should be directed mainly at the products being offered with a closer look at *one* of the large and successful companies now operating.

Question: Through an analysis on the major competitor, what is their existing product competition and what might be future competing products?

The International Market

NLI considers international marketing of its products to be similar to that of the domestic market in that there are definable and targetable areas. Assistance and cooperation from the international representatives will be necessary to ensure successful market penetration. As stated earlier, NLI will proceed with attempts to obtain foreign patents on its devices and to expand its operations worldwide as capabilities and funds become available.

Question: What actions are required to commit to the international market?

Last-Minute CEO Directive

In support of NLI's goal to quickly generate a positive cash flow, the CEO has dictated that initial marketing efforts be concentrated in segments where quick buying decisions are made and where orders are on a cash basis (credit cards, money orders, or certified funds). He considers direct sales, through trade publication advertisements and direct mail, the least costly and most lucrative methods to penetrate the market. Therefore, your initial strategies must now include direct mailing of order form/brochures and ad placements in selected automotive-related publications.

Question: Based on your data collection, what is the most lucrative publication for ad placement with mailing-list parameters that would be most desirable for inclusion in your marketing initiatives?

Related Professional Associations

Specialty Equipment Market Association (SEMA) located at www.sema.org provides information and market research on the specialty equipment and automotive aftermarket industry.

BIG MOUNTAIN CORPORATION

David Stotlar, Northern Colorado University

● ●

Descriptive Information for the Big Mountain Corporation

Big Mountain Corporation, located in a large western city, is a small to medium-sized manufacturer of consumer goods relating to hiking, backpacking, and climbing activities. It is a family-controlled organization begun about 25 years ago. Big Mountain is considering a major expansion of facilities and product lines to tap the rapidly growing and diversified market. The 5-year outlook for obtaining and developing key managerial personnel poses a problem in light of the technological changes and corporate expansion plans that would require considerable technical expertise and innovative ability. Basically, the production techniques, the products, and the consumers themselves have grown very sophisticated in the last decade. In order to maintain a competitive advantage in an industry dominated by huge companies, Big Mountain has to be extremely creative and current regarding the technology required to produce its products. The plan for modernizing and expanding existing facilities indicated that reorganization would be needed. It has been predicted that business expansion and new-product development needs would create demands for new specializations and hiring (particularly in engineering and marketing).

Currently, Big Mountain has 105 persons in managerial positions. The managers are divided among departments as shown in Table 1.

Table 1
Big Mountain Market and Production Expansion

	Number of managers	Present average salary (without 21% fringes)	Projected Increase
Executive Staff	5	$83,121	10%
Manufacturing	34	$36,065	50%
Accounting	17	$38,454	30%
Finance	6	$39,140	20%
Marketing	13	$57,900	40%
Engineering	21	$38,731	30%
Personnel	5	$36,248	20%
TOTAL	105		

The problem before you is whether Big Mountain should still plan to significantly increase its productive capacity, based on continued optimistic demand data for hiking, backpacking, and climbing products. The company will need to add human resources in some areas and perhaps decrease them in other areas within the next 2 years in order to facilitate the expansion.

Specifically, Big Mountain is considering an increase in production capacity within the next 2 years. Market research, new-product development, financial planning, personnel, production planning, and scheduling will each have to conduct independent analyses to determine if expansion is feasible and desirable at this time. The planned expansion includes additions to the engineering department for new product development and prototypes, to manufacturing for new work processes and scheduling, and to marketing for added sales capability and advertising. Of course, because new products will be designed, manufactured, and (it is hoped) sold, these areas must grow. In addition, support areas would also need to grow to serve the needs of the larger manufacturing organization.

Within the next 2 years, productive capacity could be increased by 50%. Physical facilities are already being finished to house manufacturing and administration expansion. With this expansion, the executive committee's estimate of sales 2 years from now, allowing for inflation, is $54,000,000.

The financial picture of Big Mountain has been consistently bright and improving. The organization, witnessed by the historical balance sheet (see Table 2), has a sound capital structure and relatively small debt obligations. Sales volume and net income have also increased in 8 of the last 10 years.

Additional information on Big Mountain concerns its specific departments. These are reasonably autonomous units, and their director or vice president typically has considerable authority for the departments' activities. Information about each department follows.

Manufacturing. This is the largest and most powerful department; however, the department lacks direction, as its senior people must take charge of the entire operation, and they are reluctant to delegate any authority in manufacturing, which is a reason for their failure to promote anyone to challenge their authority in the manufacturing department. Equipment is modern, but expertise in production planning and control is shallow. Ties to engineering are weak.

Accounting. Accounting is not a large group, but is professional. It boasts graduates from prestigious business schools and people from major public accounting firms. The goals of the department are to educate managers in accounting practices and set up Big Mountain as an example in the

Table 2
Historical Abbreviated Financial Data
for Big Mountain Corporation (in thousands of dollars)

Assets	Two years ago	Last year	This year
Cash	49	48	53
Marketable securities	150	165	170
Receivables, net	199	205	208
Inventories	300	310	324
Net plant and equipment	1,300	1,280	1,273
Total assets	2,000	2,008	2,028
Claims on Assets			
Accounts payable	60	59	63
Notes payable	100	97	106
Accruals	9	9	9
Federal income taxes accrued	131	135	140
Mortgage bonds	500	495	500
Stock	600	620	632
Retained earnings	600	593	578
Total claims on assets	1,998	2,008	2,028
Net sales volume	30,000	32,500	36,000
Net income (after taxes)	921	1,235	1,386

industry of an organization that is able to implement the latest accounting conventions and rules correctly and efficiently.

Finance. This department is quite small, perhaps due to the family-owned nature of the company. One member of the department is a member of the family of the founders and owners of Big Mountain. The remainder of the department consists of managers with little power.

Marketing. This department is viable and visible. It has a pool of creative people who have developed a effective sales network. Their goals are to expand and begin to develop in-house advertising capability.

Engineering. The engineering department is large, but contains many people who direct the maintenance system for machinery and other tangible assets. Liaison with the manufacturing department is poor, and this hinders morale in engineering. The best people hope for transfers to manufacturing where things actually happen. Engineering contains a small research and development (R-and-D) group who are given excellent physical resources and who are quite visible. However, their work is seldom advanced through manufacturing where the ideas for new products always seem to originate. R-and-D has been called a public-relations gimmick by some. The director of engineering was recently hired to develop the department into a viable force, particularly R-and-D, but is having problems retaining people.

Personnel. Personnel is the smallest department as far as number of managers, but has several clerks because of its record-keeping functions. Personnel is involved in an affirmative-action program, in union negotiations, and in contract administration almost exclusively. Selection and training are primarily decentralized (i.e., left to line managers). Performance appraisal and career development are the department's strong points.

Case Problem

The decision being considered is the addition of a third shift to join the existing two (hence the 50% increase in manufacturing). Assume a span of control from management to labor at 1 to 5 with an average salary for labor at $21,000 with fringe benefits at 18%. Inflation will exist at 5% per year across the board.

Your task is to determine if market and production expansion is warranted within the stated parameters. Will the increased labor costs be covered by the increase in sales (it will be assumed that all other expense data remain fixed)? Is this a wise move for Big Mountain Corporation? Justify your answer.

Suggested Readings

Blankenship, A. B., & Breen, G. (1995). *State of the art marketing research*. Chicago: American Marketing Association.

Breen, G., & Blankenship, A. B. (1989). *Do-it-yourself marketing research*. New York: McGraw-Hill.

Cohen, W. A. (1991). *The practice of marketing management*. New York: Macmillan.

Author's Note: A solution for Big Mountain is presented in Table 3.

Table 3
Solution for Big Mountain Case

		Avg. Salary	Total Salary		Expansion	New Avg. Salary	Total Salary
Executive Staff	5	$83,121	$415,605		5	$87,277	$436,385
Accounting	17	$38,454	$653,718		22	$40,377	$888,287
Manufacturing	34	$36,065	$1,226,210		51	$37,868	$1,931,281
Finance	6	$39,140	$234,840		7	$41,097	$287,679
Marketing	13	$57,900	$752,700		18	$60,795	$1,094,310
Engineering	21	$38,731	$813,351		27	$40,668	$1,098,024
Personnel	5	$36,248	$181,240		6	$38,060	$228,362
			$4,277,664		$346,142	$5,964,329	
Fringes at .21			$5,175,973	Total Cost Mgmt	Fringes at .21		$7,216,838
Work force	505	$21,000	$10,605,000		680	$22,050	$14,994,000
Fringes at .18			$12,513,900	Total Cost Labor	Fringes at .18		$17,692,920
	Total Personnel Costs		$17,689,873			Total Personnel Costs	$24,909,758
	Old Sales Vol.		$36,000,000			New Sales Vol.	$54,000,000
				Net gain Sales		$18,000,000	
				Net Pers. Exp. Increase		$7,219,884	
				Difference		$10,780,116	
				With $10 million increase, they should expand.			

FOOTBALL HELMETS AND THE CONCUSSION DILEMMA

Wayne Blann, Ithaca College

Background

In a December 19, 1994, *Sports Illustrated* article by Peter King titled "Halt the Head Hunting," Buffalo Bills defensive end Bruce Smith said of pass rushing: "It's an art. It's also a car accident" (p. 29). King also reported on how Los Angeles Rams defensive end Fred Stokes felt about plowing through Atlanta Falcons quarterback Jeff George after he released the ball. Stokes said, "It sounds animalistic but I got such a rush, I was slobbering. That's the game. It might be crazy, but it goes back to Pop Warner football. At every level, the harder you hit, the more you get patted on the back and the happier you are" (p. 29). According to King, that is the culture of the game. Data supplied by the 28 National Football League teams showed that 445 concussions were suffered by 341 players between 1989 and 1993. This represents about four concussions per weekend and about 2.5 concussions for every 1,000 plays. King reported other evidence that indicates that concussions are the silent epidemic of football:

- 250,000 out of 1.5 million high school football players suffer concussions during any given season
- Players who have already suffered concussions are four times more likely to suffer another concussion than players who have not suffered concussions
- Concussions are under-reported at all levels of football because players do not admit to the injuries and trainers cannot readily diagnose mild concussions
- NFL guidelines for allowing players to return to play after suffering concussions are too lenient and in some cases more lenient than professional boxing's guidelines
- Post concussion syndrome among NFL players and former players is more widespread than believed because players do not want to admit to their conditions." (pp. 40, 45)

The Effects of Hard-Hitting in Football

Football is a contact sport that involves clean, hard hitting, but it should not allow cheap shots, unnecessary or intentionally rough hits to be carried out by players against other players. Allowing unnecessary rough hits by players increases the chances that players will suffer from concussions. Neuropsychologists agree that individuals who have concussions tend to have more concussions, more easily, and that repeated insults to the brain cause neuropsychological damage. However, little information exists regarding the effects of football concussions at any level in the game. Neither administrators, coaches, athletic trainers, nor players really want to know what effects concussions have had on players or the extent to which players have incurred neurological problems.

Developing A Marketing Plan

The manufacturers of the padded football helmets recognize that their product might be better than existing helmets in protecting players from suffering concussions from some hard hits. The evidence that exists about concussions suffered by football players clearly allows the manufacturers an opportunity to market the padded helmets as a "safety precaution" for all players, at all levels of the game. However, the manufacturers also recognize that marketing the padded helmets solely on the basis that they provide a "safety precaution" for players ignores the ethical issues that exist within the context of the culture of the game and society (i.e, encouraging, endorsing, and even cheering violence). Indeed, the manufacturers believe that if players think their product better protects them from concussions, they will try to hit even harder, because the culture of the game values such tactics.

Historically, as the sports equipment manufacturing industry develops improved protective equipment, other kinds of player injuries emerge as a result of the new equipment. The record shows that sports equipment manufacturers are ultimately sued by players for injuries they incur that are linked to protective sports equipment. Given this reality, it is likely that manufacturing, marketing, and selling the new padded football helmets might result in product liability lawsuits. Consequently, the manufacturers might also confront this product liability issue.

The manufacturers recognize they have both a legal and ethical responsibility to properly protect players' health in the long term, not simply make them somewhat better protected (possibly) from concussions in the short term.

The manufacturers realize that marketing their product on the basis that it provides players better protection from concussions fails to address the causes of the problem that threatens players' health in the long term. The manufacturers believe they have a social responsibility to market their product in ways that will help change not only the rules of the game but also, indeed, the culture of the game. It is their perspective that a marketing plan for padded helmets must include strategies that will encourage football governing bodies and rules committees to take actions that will actually reduce, if not eliminate, the incidence of player concussions in the game.

The manufacturers of the padded football helmets decided to consult with sport marketing experts (you and your classmates) to develop a marketing plan that addresses the ethical issues involved in this situation and that, when implemented, will result in the product's being marketed in socially responsible ways. The manufacturers have requested that you develop a marketing proposal that (a) establishes a clear mission, (b) identifies specific objectives derived from the mission, (c) sets forth marketing strategies that reach targeted audiences at all levels of the game and will carry out the objectives and mission, (d) clearly identifies the ethical issues that exist in the culture of the game and in society and how they influence the marketing strategies, and (e) demonstrates the ways in which the marketing plan addresses the ethical issues and is socially responsible.

Questions for Study

1. Discuss the legal issues in the game of football that relate to this marketing problem.
2. Discuss the ethical issues in the game of football that relate to this marketing problem.
3. Write a marketing mission statement.
4. Write specific marketing objectives derived from and linked to the mission statement.
5. Describe specific marketing/promotions programs/activities that might be implemented to reach specific target audiences in carrying out the marketing objectives and to achieve the marketing mission statement.
6. Explain how the marketing plan you recommend be implemented will address the legal and ethical issues in the game of football.

Suggested Readings

Blann, F.W. (1998). Sport marketing. In J. B. Parks, B. R. K. Zanger, & J. Quarterman (Eds.), *Contemporary sport management* (pp. 171–184). Champaign, IL: Human Kinetics.

Covey, S. R. (1989). *The seven habits of highly effective people.* New York: Simon and Schuster.

Grunig, J. E., & White, R. (1992). Communication, public relations and effective organizations. In J. E. Grunig (Ed.), *Excellence in public relations and communications management*. Hillsdale, NJ: Erlbaum.

Slack, T. (1997). *Understanding sport organizations: The application of organizational theory*. Champaign IL: Human Kinetics.

Related Professional Associations

American Marketing Association
250 South Wacker Drive, Suite 200
Chicago, IL 60606
(800)AMA-1150
http://www.ama.org

National Collegiate Athletic Association
6201 College Boulevard
Overland Park, KS 66211-2422
(913)339-1906
http://www.ncaa.org

National Football League
http://www.nfl.com

National Football League Players Association
http://www.sportsline.com/u/NFLPlayers

Sporting Goods Manufacturers Association
200 Castlewood Drive
North Palm Beach, FL 33408
(561)842-4100
http://www.sportlink.com

ADIDAS: MAKING A COMEBACK

Dianna P. Gray, University of Northern Colorado

Background

Adidas had its beginnings in the 1920s, in Herzogenaurach, Germany, shortly after the end of World War I, when Adi Dassler and his brother, Rudolf, began making athletic shoes especially for runners and soccer players. Adi Dassler realized that to be credible with consumers, his product must be credible with athletes. By the 1950s, Adidas, so named for Adi Dassler's first and last names, had established an image as the premier athletic footwear company. This image was created primarily by the number of track and field athletes who won Olympic medals in Dassler's shoes, the most notable being American Jesse Owens, who won an unprecedented four gold medals at the 1936 Berlin Olympic Games. This early success established Adidas as a market leader in the athletic footwear industry and, by the 1970s, helped turn the firm into the world's top athletic shoe company.

Although Adidas invented the modern athletic shoe and dominated the industry for many years, it has fallen from its leadership position in the last two decades. After Adi Dassler's death in 1978, the company, faced with increased competition from U.S.-based companies Nike and Reebok, and more recently, Fila, has struggled. Adidas' philosophy of making excellent shoes for real athletes was compromised during the 1970s when the trend of athletic shoes as fashion statements for "weekend warriors" emerged. Slow to react to market changes, and badly underestimating the U.S. market, Adidas was left in the marketing dust of Nike, which, by emphasizing research and development, aggressive marketing, and shifting manufacturing to the Far East, was able to bring new products to the marketplace more quickly and cheaply than Adidas did. Once the market leader, Adidas fell to fourth in the U.S. athletic shoe market (see Table 1).

Though Adidas remained relatively strong in the international markets, its shoe sales in the United States lagged behind. In an effort to strengthen its U.S. position, in 1986 Adidas AG created Adidas USA, Inc., by buying out the four independent Adidas distributorships in the United States. The consolidation of the U.S. distributors was an important move by Adidas if it expected to make inroads in the $8 billion U.S. market, where more than half of the world's athletic shoe sales occur.

In 1990, with the company still struggling and faced with the death of Horst Dassler, Adi's son and Adidas CEO, the Dasslers sold the company to

Table 1
Percentage of U.S. Athletic Shoe Market, 1990

Company	Percent of Total US Market
Nike	33%
Reebok	24%
L.A. Gear	12%
Adidas	2%
Converse	2%

Source: *USA Today*. 1991

French corporate raider Bernard Tapie. For a brief period, things began to look up. In 1991 a new line of performance-oriented functional shoes and apparel, called Equipment, was developed, and company executives began to feel more optimistic about the chances of gaining in the U.S. market. In 1993, Adidas America was created, and along with its parent, Adidas AG, was purchased by an investment group, led by Robert Louis-Dreyfus. Louis-Dreyfus, former head of the British advertising group Saatchi & Saatchi, felt that only a couple of changes were needed to turn the company around.

How did Adidas lose its commanding lead in the athletic footwear market and get to its current status? What can Adidas do to try and recapture market share and bolster a sagging brand image? A review of Adidas, past and current marketing strategies should shed some light on this situation.

Marketing Strategy

The marketing strategies pioneered by Adidas influenced the entire athletic footwear industry. By having Olympic athletes wear Adidas products during international competition, the ultimate testing ground for its athletic footwear, the company received tremendous visibility and was able to obtain feedback from athletes, which led to continuous design changes and improvements. Endorsement contracts were made with the national sports associations, rather than with individual athletes, as is the case now. It is because of Adidas' early use of endorsement contracts that now virtually every athlete, Olympic and professional alike, has an endorsement contract with a footwear company. College players, and in some cases high school players, drafted by the National Basketball Association end up with lucrative endorsement contracts before they have played a single professional game!

In addition to its success with Olympic athletes, early in its history, Adidas established itself as the foremost provider of quality soccer shoes for elite players. The company is responsible for the development of several advances in soccer-shoe technology. The 1954 German team won the World Cup wearing Adidas shoes, and little has changed since to challenge the company's dominance in soccer.

To establish an easily recognized brand image, Adidas developed and marketed its distinctive, three stripes logo. It is essential for the effectiveness of endorsement contracts that the company's logo (mark) be easily recognized by fans and potential customers. This is the primary reason for paying an athlete to wear a particular product: Customers who see the product worn by an elite athlete want to associate with the athlete's success or image by wearing the same shoe. Another benefit of a highly recognizable and distinctive logo is its use with other product lines, such as equipment, apparel, and related products.

During the late 1970s and early 1980s, Adidas led the athletic footwear industry in offering the widest variety of running shoes. Shoes for every type of foot and running style — more than a hundred styles and models — made up Adidas' inventory. Only Nike would later eclipse Adidas in the number of styles and models of running shoes offered.

Where Did Adidas Go Wrong?

How could a company with such a commanding share of the athletic footwear market in 1980 and, on the face of it, a successful marketing strategy, let its market advantage slip away? Without doubt, Adidas underestimated both the potential growth of the athletic shoe market (in the late 1970s and early 1980s) and Nike's aggressiveness in seeking to dominate the U.S. marketplace. Adidas enjoyed many years of relatively little competition in the United States, and it was not until Nike and Reebok exploited the fitness craze of the 1970s that Adidas was faced with any significant rivals. Certainly, Adidas' slow recognition of the market conditions in the United States is evidence of marketing myopia.

Clearly the barriers to entering the market were not insurmountable, as Nike and Reebok, and a host of other smaller firms demonstrated. Neither the technology nor the money needed to begin production was enough to prevent a number of competing companies from entering the market. Should not Adidas have been more aware of this fact? Why did the company not aggressively discourage the development of competing companies by expanding the channels of distribution and adding retail outlets?

There were, however, other factors besides Nike's emergence in the athletic footwear industry that contributed to Adidas' undoing, not the least of which were its high production costs. Most of Adidas shoes were produced in Germany and France, where labor costs were considerably higher than if the company manufactured its shoes in the Far East. In addition, there were distribution problems faced by the company's four U.S.-based distributorships. Many retailers lost confidence in the company when it did not fulfill orders in a timely fashion.

However, the main problem probably was that the company lost its focus on products made for serious athletes. The move away from catering to the serious athletes and diversifying into fashion proved disastrous.

Making a Comeback

Since Louis-Dreyfus' arrival as CEO, he has pared staff drastically and doubled the marketing spending to 11% of sales, realizing that running shoes are running shoes, and image is all (Levine, 1996). Another Louis-Dreyfus move was to sell Adidas' factories in Europe and move production to the Far East, where most of the factories that manufacture athletic shoes exist. The result was the outsourcing of all production and the creation of a new logistics department to manage these new business relationships in Asia.

Another change in Adidas strategy was to reduce the number of product lines it offered. Historically the company produced shoes and apparel for every conceivable sport. As mentioned previously, at one time the company offered the second-largest selection of running shoes — over a hundred different styles and models — exceeded only by Nike. By eliminating the production of some items, particularly those with low demand, and focusing on the production of high-demand shoes, profitability has increased.

Under Louis-Dreyfus, the company is also refocusing and concentrating again on developing footwear for athletes. Adidas' heritage, successfully copied by Nike, is one of innovating and designing performance products. Adidas is returning to its original positioning as a company that makes products for the serious athlete. Adidas is also heavily involved in sponsorship as part of its sport marketing strategy. Table 2 lists Adidas' various sponsorship commitments.

In an effort to deal with the shipping and on-time delivery problems, issues that have historically plagued Adidas, sourcing and distribution have been restructured. Like other athletic footwear manufacturers, Adidas ships product from the factory to a regional warehouse before shipment to local retailers. Improved logistics, along with better relations with the factory,

Table 2
Adidas' Sponsorship Activities

Event	Sport/Level	Sponsorship Level
National High School Coaches Assn. National Basketball Championship	Amateur	Sponsor
NASCAR Winston Cup Series	Auto Sports	Associate Car Sponsor
Adidas/MetLife Soccer Classic at Indiana University	College	Title Sponsor
National Cycle League	Cycling	Sponsor
Boston Marathon (Official Footwear & Apparel)	Endurance	Official Sponsor
U.S. Soccer USA Boxing U.S. Weightlifting	Olympic	Official Sponsor
World Cup USA 1994	Soccer/International	Official Sponsor
U.S. Soccer	Olympic	Official Sponsor
U.S. Amateur Soccer Association	Soccer/Amateur	Title Sponsor: Adidas U.S. Open Cup
ATP Senior Tour	Tennis	Official Sponsor Sponsor: Thriftway ATP Championship

Source: *Sports Sponsor Fact Book (1995)*

better quality control, and more timely delivery from the factory to the warehouse, has improved the company's delivery record and helped change retailers' attitudes toward the company and its products.

Adidas has also made a commitment to increased marketing of its products and the restoration of its brand image. The company was founded on the philosophy of making superior shoes for elite athletes. Nike, however, with Michael Jordan as its prime endorser, has taken the athletic footwear market to new levels. Adidas' reputation as the footwear of choice for professional and elite athletes has been usurped by Nike, particularly in the U.S. market, and Nike continues to gain market share internationally. It will be difficult for Adidas to return to its former status as the industry leader in athletic footwear, no matter how many marketing dollars the company is willing to spend in its fight against Nike and Reebok.

In an effort to capture some of the youth and Generation X markets, Adidas is placing a greater emphasis on grassroots activities and focusing some of its advertising on attracting teenaged, urban consumers away from the established Nike and Reebok brands. Rather than focus its marketing efforts solely on top-level, big-dollar marketing tactics, Adidas is doing a lot of guerrilla marketing activities at the lower levels of sports. An event that has attracted considerable attention outside the United States is a 3-on-3 outdoor basketball tournament, developed to give youngsters in Europe, South America, Africa, and Asia an opportunity to compete with each other. The first world championships were held in 1995 in Barcelona. Over 200,000 people were on hand during the 2-day event to watch teams from 51 countries compete.

Because the company cannot compete head-on with the marketing and advertising expenditures of Nike and Reebok, Adidas has decided to target key metropolitan areas in the United States, rather than attempt to blanket the entire country. New York City and Miami were identified as prime areas. Subway car cards and graffiti-style painted walls are among the advertising tactics being used to build up Adidas' brand image, particularly among the 12-24 demographic.

Conclusion

Even though Adidas has not regained its previous position as the most respected brand of athletic footwear, it is making a comeback. From less than 2% of the U.S. market in 1991, to approximately 6.5% in 1997, Adidas is gradually making up lost ground.

Table 3
Percentage of U.S. Athletic Shoe Market, 1995

Company	Percent of Total US Market
Nike	36.8%
Reebok	20.5%
Adidas	6.2%
Fila	5.8%
Keds	3.6%
Converse	2.9%

Source: *USA Today*, September 17, 1996, p. 3B

Six and a half percent may not seem like much, especially when compared with Nike's 36.8%. However, with the U.S. market accounting for over half of the $14 billion world market, a shift of four percentage points can mean nearly a quarter billion dollars of incremental sales.

Furthermore, according to analysts, the trend should continue. The projected growth for Adidas in the U.S. is 8% by 1998. On top of that, Adidas continues to be a dominant player internationally, based primarily on its leadership position in Germany, Japan, and Argentina, as well as its dominance in the rapidly growing Eastern European markets.

Case Study Questions

What happened in U.S. markets during the 1960s and 1970s that later had a profound impact on Adidas' market share?

Why did Adidas lose its commanding position in the U.S. athletic footwear market? Could this have been prevented? How?

What should Adidas have done to protect its market position from competing companies, Nike, Reebok, and L.A. Gear?

How has Adidas regained its brand image and become a competitive player in the U.S. athletic footwear market? What would you recommend Adidas do to continue its comeback? Would you build on the current strategies or recommend new ones? Justify your recommendations.

Related Activities

1. You can find Adidas on the World Wide Web at http://www.adidas.com. Periodically check their income statement (at http://www.adidas.com/finance/financial.htm) to see if the company is continuing its comeback.

2. Where is Adidas ranked currently with respect to its percentage of the U.S. shoe market? The international shoe market?

3. Compare Adidas' 1995 sponsorship activities (Table 2) with its current sponsorship commitments. Has Adidas changed the sports it is targeting? What does this tell you about Adidas' marketing strategy?

4. Conduct some focus group research with a group of 10 to 15 students on your campus to determine the level of brand recognition and loyalty for different footwear and apparel companies. You might compare Nike, Adidas, Reebok, Fila, and Converse. Use your findings to help determine how you would continue Adidas' comeback.

Related Readings

Carter, D. M. (1996). *Keeping score: An inside look at sports marketing.*

Grants Pass, OR: The Oasis Press.

Friedman, A. (1995). *Sports sponsor fact book*. Chicago, IL: Team Marketing Report.

Gwin, P. (1996, June). Adidas jumps back into the race. *Europe, 357,* 22–24.

Gelsi, S. (1995, December 4). Sneaking into third. *Brandweek, 36,* 24–25.

Hartley, R. F. (1986). Adidas — Letting market advantage slip away. In *Marketing mistakes* (3rd ed.). New York: John Wiley & Sons.

Jensen, J. (1994, July 25). Adidas continues to play hard. *Advertising Age, 65,* 42.

Jones, D. (1996, September 17). Nike orders secure industry foothold. *USA Today,* p. 3B.

Kindel, S. (1996, February). Making a run for the money: Adidas AG. *Hemispheres,* 47–48, 50.

Mussey, D. (1995, February 13). Adidas strides on its own path. *Advertising Age, 66,* 6.

Pitts, B. G., & Stotlar, D. K. (1996). *Fundamentals of sport marketing.* Morgantown, WV: Fitness Information Technology, Inc.

Schaaf, P. (1995). *Sports marketing: It's not just a game anymore.* Amherst, NY: Prometheus Books.

Schlossberg, H. (1996). *Sports marketing.* Cambridge, MA: Blackwell Publishers, Inc.

Sandomir, R. (1996, May 22). Bryant a pitchman before he's a pro. *The New York Times,* pp. B9, B13.

Strasser, J. B., & Becklund, L. (1991). *Swoosh: The unauthorized story of Nike and the men who played there.* New York: Harcourt Brace Jovanovich, Publishers.

Sullivan, R. (1996, July). Sneaker wars. *Vogue, 186,* 138–141, 173.

Suggested Trade Newsletters and Publications

Advertising Age   *Marketing News*
Adweek   *New Product News*
American Demographics   *Sports Business Daily*
Brandweek   *Team Marketing Report*
Consumer Reports

References

Levine, J. (1996, March 25). Adidas flies again. *Forbes, 157,* 44–45.

SECTION 3

THE SPORT PROMOTION INDUSTRY SEGMENT

The Sport Promotion Industry Segment: An Overview

There are products needed or desired for the purpose of promoting a sport product. Therefore, any product — goods, services, people, places, or ideas — created for the function of promotion fits into this industry segment. This part of the sport industry is composed of products that are used as promotional tools to sell products in the sport industry. Sports team souvenir T-shirts fall into this category. Advertising is in this category. Advertising is a product to be sold. Therefore, if a fitness center wants to advertise its products, it must purchase advertising.

Promotional methods in the sport industry include a large variety of products. This includes souvenirs, pregame giveaways, endorsement advertising, sponsorship, and media relations.

Sports is also a promotional tool used by companies to sell their products. In other words, there are businesses that use sports as an advertising tool. Therefore, many sports businesses must consider their sports events in this way — how the sports event can be used to help sell another product. This usually comes in the form of sponsorship or endorsement. Here are some examples. A cereal company puts a famous athlete's picture on the cereal box hoping that more cereal will be sold. This is called endorsement advertising. The athlete's picture suggests that the athlete supports, or endorses, the cereal. In another example, a prestigious car company helps fund a professional women's golf tournament. This is sponsorship. The car company is suggesting the notion that those who drive the car participate in or are fans of a prestigious sport. The company is attempting to appeal to the consumers of the event and of the sport.

The cases in this section involve promotional products — those products used to promote a sport product. Refer to chapters 11–15 in the Pitts and Stotlar (1996) textbook for help.

THE SINKING OF THE AMERICA'S CUP

David Stotlar, Northern Colorado University

● ●

Sponsoring sporting events has gained popularity in the past several years as corporations attempt to break through advertising clutter. Considerable attention is focused on successful campaigns, but not all sponsorship deals provide the result anticipated by event owners or corporate sponsors. The following report from the IEG Sponsorship Report (June 1, 1992, reprinted with permission) chronicles some of the problems encountered during a sponsored sailing event.

America's Cup Players

America's Cup Organizing Committee (ACOC): Responsible for defending Cup and staging event. Formed from Sail America Foundation, which ran Dennis Conner's '87 and '88 Cup efforts. Prohibited by a self-imposed "defense plan" from selling sponsorship to commercial entities until October 1990. Finishes race with $11 million in sponsorship and $3 million in debt. Major sponsors: San Diego Unified Port District, AT&T, Coors Brewing Co. and TGI Friday's Inc.

Malin Burnham: ACOC president, San Diego banker and San Diego Yacht Club (SDYC) member and former commodore. Founder of Sail America. Lent $4 million to ACOC, forgiving $2 million in '91.

Tom Ehman: San Diego Yacht Club (SDYC) member tapped by Burnham as ACOC executive vice president/general manager. Executive director of New York Yacht Club's (NYYC) America II challenge in 1986–87.

David McGuigan: ACOC vice president marketing; former head of IMG's Chicago office and former vice president of sales at Dennis Conner Sports. Hired IMG and Arlen Marketing.

Ernie Taylor: Executive director of the Challenger of Record Committee (CORC) that conducted the America's Cup challenger races.

International Management Group (IMG): Agency that has represented Conner's personal licensing and merchandising since '87. TV subsidiary TWI won contact to advise on and sell ACOC TV rights. Hired by ACOC to sell international licensing. Later retained to sell ACOC sponsorship in joint venture with Arlen Marketing.

Arlen Marketing: Agency hired to sell ACOC domestic licensing. Formed joint venture with IMG to sell ACOC sponsorship. Headed by former Dennis Conner Sports executive vice president Doug Augustine.

Marketing and Promotion Group: Agency hired by McGuigan to manage $1 million America's Cup Village (a special event and tourist festival center built and run in conjunction with the America's Cup Event) during May 1991 Int'l America's Cup Class World Championships.

The Omnis Co.: Hired by ACOC on Arlen/IMG's recommendation in October 1991 to manage America's Cup International Centre (for hospitality and tourism). Fired by ACOC in March 1992, when Arlen/IMG took over management.

Team Dennis Conner: Syndicate that raised $10.5 million in sponsorship, led by American Airlines, General Motors Corp.'s Cadillac Motor Car Division and Pepsi-Cola Co., which anteed up to $3 million each.

America 3: Syndicate formed by multimillionaire Bill Koch that set sail with $6 million in sponsorship, primarily from Coors Brewing Co., General Motors' Corvette, AT&T and Digital Equipment Corp., each of which spent $500,000 to $1.5 million. Successfully defended the Cup in May 1992.

In the Beginning

From a historical standpoint, the America's Cup has been embroiled in controversy since its inception. In 1851 New York business leaders were invited to send a New York harbor pilot boat to London to participate in the World Trade Exhibition. In responding, the Commodore of the New York Yacht Club, built an extremely fast boat for the event and christened it "America." The race victory for America brought the Royal Squadron Cup to the United States and it has been known as the America's Cup ever since. Significant legal battles over the America's Cup continued from 1871 through the 1983 series with arguments over the design and length of challenger's ships and race schedules. It was in 1983 that U.S. skipper Dennis Conner lost the Cup to Australia II of the Royal Perth Yacht Club. The succeeding race in 1987 off the shores of Perth brought additional turmoil. Considerable discussion occurred over the ownership of the television rights for the Cup race with the Royal Perth Yacht Club (as owner of the Cup) eventually coming out in control. However, the series, through the efforts of Dennis Connor and the crew of the Stars and Stripes, brought the Cup and its controversies back to the United States and the San Diego Yacht

Club. This is where the current case study of the 1992 America's Cup event begins.

As the America's Cup Organizing Committee faced a $3 million debt and a bevy of unhappy sponsors in the wake of its 1992 event, preparing for 1995 seemed to be the least of its problems.

Debt and discontent stemmed from a string of missteps by ACOC. Among them:

- Badly misreading the sponsorship market
- Relying on overly optimistic forecasts of income from TV rights fees, then losing those rights when a cash crunch hampered its ability to cover TV production costs.
- Overestimating the number of potential attendees and the event's economic impact.

"From the beginning, ACOC didn't understand how to package the event and sell it to corporate America," said Mary Reiling, staff manager, national event marketing for AT&T, the low-seven-figure presenting sponsor of ACOC's America's Cup Int'l Centre. "Once we signed on, it was evident that although ACOC and San Diego Yacht Club could run the races, they did not know how to run an event. We did not receive the value we expected."

"After we came aboard and started asking questions, we saw ACOC didn't have the infrastructure to handle it," said Paul Leroue, Coors Brewing Co.'s assistant brand manager, Coors Light, which sponsored the Centre and eventual defender America.

Sponsors who refused the organizing committee's proposals say they did so after sensing potential problems. "We're not the least bit surprised things didn't turn out the way ACOC wanted," said Ladd Biro, director, world-wide sales promotion for American Airlines, which turned down ACOC in favor of renewing with Team Dennis Conner. "The organization was not particularly well run. We felt it was better to steer clear, and I'm glad we did."

Packaged Goods

Disgruntled sponsors were the last thing ACOC president Malin Burnham and executive vice president Tom Ehman expected to confront. "Our number-one goal was to defend the Cup, and the best way to do that was to see that the syndicates were funded, so we decided not to sell sponsorship," said Tom Mitchell, ACOC's senior vice president of operations.

The event's "defense plan" gave the syndicates first crack at sponsor dol-

lars and prohibited ACOC from seeking backers until October 1990, and
then only with its board's approval. Instead, ACOC's $33 million budget was
to come from TV rights fees-projected at $22 million — as well as license
agreements, in-kind commitments, memberships and merchandise sales.

However, supporting a syndicate was not ideal for every potential sponsor. Tying into the right syndicate might offer a windfall of on-camera visibility, but tying into a loser meant watching investment sail out of view.

"Why spend money backing the wrong horse?" said Warner Canto, senior vice president, worldwide marketing development, American Express
TRS Co (AmEx).

Faced with that dilemma in 1987, AmEx sought to guarantee presence
with whichever syndicate ended up defending the Cup in 1988. It offered
six syndicates a total of $750,000, with the largest portion earmarked for the
top finisher. The syndicates, cutthroat competitors on land and sea, would
not cooperate. "One called a press conference denouncing the whole thing,"
Canto said. "We pulled the program."

Leading up to this year's event, potential sponsors again pushed for a
sponsorship program that made sense for them. Many turned to ACOC in
hopes of a unified Cup package. "From day one, we told ACOC we wanted
the event, not the syndicates," Reiling said. "It wouldn't put together the
package for us." Even some within the America's Cup camp pushed to con-
solidate competing interests by developing a package that would have included syndicate and event sponsorship, as well as ad time on event TV
broadcasts.

"I was in Ehman's office three years ago and said 'Let's market this to-
gether,' " said Ernie Taylor, executive director of the Challenger of Record
Committee (CORC), which conducted the America's Cup challenger races.
"He said, 'Yeah, yeah, sure,' and went off and did all these deals without us."

Unplugged

ACOC retained Trans World Int'l, the broadcast arm of IMG, to sell the
event's foreign TV rights and consult on the sale of domestic rights. In October 1990, ACOC struck a deal with ESPN: $3 million for U.S. broadcast
rights and another $5 million toward production.

Although Taylor said ACOC did not consult with CORC until the ESPN
deal was signed, the committees agreed to share subsequent production
risks and rewards on a 55-45 basis in anticipation of TWI's projected $14.5
million in foreign rights. By May 1991, immediately after ACOC staged the
Int'l America's Cup Class World Championships, the joint TV deal began to

unravel. Excessive production costs put ACOC $2.6 million over budget and overseas rights fees were slow in coming.

"We expected most of the rights payments to come in up front," Burnham said. "Instead, they came in at the end. TWI honestly made cash flow estimates it thought were right, but the economy slid, and I know TWI had difficulty selling foreign rights."

"In June '91, we couldn't get proper accounting from ACOC," Taylor said. "Finally it admitted that more than $1 million that was supposed to be used for TV production had been spent on other areas of the event."

In July, Burnham fired off a letter to CORC nixing the agreement, leaving ACOC holding all TV rights-and risks, Taylor said. As ACOC's cash flow deteriorated, it approached CORC in October and again in November to reinstate the agreement. Taylor refused.

By December, ACOC admitted it could not fund TV production, Taylor said. On Jan. 24, ACOC forfeited broadcast rights to CORC and TWI. The new partners, who then sold $5 million in foreign rights, made it an 80-20 split, minus ACOC's debts.

Village People

Early in '91, ACOC decided to use the 10-day Worlds to "test public interest" in an America's Cup Village, Burnham said. ACOC vice president of marketing Dave McGuigan retained John Peterson, president of Marketing and Promotion Group, to "organize the Village for the Worlds, and if it worked out, to do it for the Cup," Mitchell said. Peterson said his contract extended through May 1992.

Despite the self-imposed ban on sponsorship, in October 1990, ACOC landed an "up to" $8.3 million Village sponsorship from the San Diego Unified Port District, which, as a noncommercial entity, was exempt from the ban.

However, Port District authorities who did not return calls from IEG Sponsorship Report, released funds slowly-and on the condition that they not be used to promote the village, Burnham said. "The district is a quasi-governmental body; we had to operate within the parameters of its legal and political policy."

In lieu of promotion dollars, "Peterson had to work with local radio stations to set up special days in the Village that the stations would promote," Mitchell said. In the end, Peterson's anticipated paid attendance of 100,000 and a $1.7 million net windfall for ACOC never materialized. Even though ACOC eliminated the gate charge, no more than 60,000 people came,

Mitchell said. "We decided we didn't know how to do a Village."

"We overdid it by having an international Village with food and cultural attractions," Burnham said. "The location was not good. It was hard to see, hard to park." Despite these problems, Burnham said he felt "a moral obligation" to build the venue on Port District property.

Death Throes

In August 1991, ACOC was $5 million in debt, despite Burnham having forgiven a $2 million personal loan. It laid off seven of 25 staff members, reduced its budget to $20 million and canceled plans for opening and closing extravaganzas.

In August, ACOC also publicly announced its search for sponsors-to the American syndicates' chagrin — through a joint venture between Arlen Marketing and IMG. ACOC had hired the two firms in August 1990 to sell domestic and international licensing, respectively.

Yet at least two sponsors told IEG Sponsorship Report they had been approached by McGuigan in early 1991 with behind-the-scenes proposals. Russell J. Ford, manager, special market promotions for American Airlines, said ACOC contacted him in January, just as the carrier was preparing to sign with Conner.

"Anything ACOC offered either duplicated Conner or wasn't worth anything to us," Ford said. "We tried to ensure that no other airline ambushed us, and as goodwill we offered to set up travel arrangements to defray expenses a little, but what ACOC was proposing was ridiculous. It needed tickets everywhere. The committee talked about hospitality and logos and PR, but we were already doing hospitality with Dennis' people."

Reiling said ACOC approached AT&T in April 1991. After she requested the syndicates' input, the committee returned with a proposal approved by America and Team Dennis Conner — not quite an umbrella package, but enough to bring her back to the table.

Meanwhile, in an attempt to find a viable sponsor hook, Arlen/IMG convinced ACOC to revive the Village concepts as the America's Cup International Centre. But the proposal lacked specifics, Canto said. "It didn't have anything for us." The Centre's eventual sponsors were dissatisfied even before the venue opened.

For example, The Omnis Co., which Arlen/IMG hired to run the Centre, sent AT&T scrambling to meet a January deadline for delivery of a 90-foot painting that would serve as the site's centerpiece. When Omnis reversed and asked AT&T to delay delivery, Reiling refused.

AT&T was no happier after the Centre opened. "It would have worked for us if attendance had been better," Reiling said. "The crowds didn't start coming until May 9, when the finals began."

ACOC also failed to provide the hospitality it promised AT&T, Reiling said. "We arranged our own and received buoy signage in exchange. Visually, the Centre didn't end up looking like we expected."

Another Centre sponsor, TGI Friday's Inc., went so far as to withhold payment, charging that Omnis failed to insure the venue. James Ishii, Omnis' chief executive, denied the charge, attributing appearances to the contrary to untimely withdrawals and deposits.

The TGI Friday's sent Arlen/IMG a letter outlining conditions for resuming payment, said Arlen president Doug Augustine. "Friday's was disappointed and felt Omnis had to go," Mitchell said. "I went to Friday's headquarters for a week and came to the same conclusion. When I came back, I recommended we cancel Omnis's license." TGI Friday's would not comment on the incident.

Arlen/IMG took over the Centre in March, Augustine said, "to maintain a relationship with sponsors, so we could see as best we could that they got everything they bargained for."

Economic Bust

Along with ACOC's internal economic woes, its event delivered just one-half to one-third of its projected economic impact on San Diego. A May 1990 University of San Diego study commissioned by ACOC estimated that the event would add $911 million to local coffers, but the total likely will be $300 million to $500 million, Mitchell said.

"We've been accused of overhyping the event and failing miserably in attracting people," Burnham said. "But whether it's $500 million or $350 million, that's $500 million or $350 million San Diego wouldn't have had. Previously, the largest event the city hosted was the Super Bowl, which I think had an impact of $131 million. We didn't do too bad."

ACOC remains $3 million in debt, including another $2 million owed to Burnham, Mitchell said. "We have no plans to file for bankruptcy."

*Material reprinted from IEG Sponsorship Report June 1, 1992 with permission from Rick G. Karr, Senior Editor. For additional information or subscriptions contact:

IEG Sponsorship Report
640 North LaSalle, Suite 600
Chicago, IL 60610-3777

Study Questions

1. In chronological order, what were the major errors committed by ACOC, and what actions could have taken to prevent them?
2. What were the major errors committed by organizers of the Village, and what actions could have taken to prevent them?
3. What basic marketing principles were violated (or ignored) by the various parties involved in sponsorship of the America's Cup Challenge?
4. Divide into small groups. Review the situation above. Your group is to present three errors made by the parties involved and identify an alternative course of action for each error that would have produced more desirable results.

Related Association

International Events Group
640 North LaSalle, Suite 600
Chicago, IL 60610-3777

Suggested Readings

IEG Sponsorship Report
International Events Group
640 North LaSalle, Suite 600
Chicago, IL 60610-3777

Other information available at
www.sponsorship.com

NATIONAL EXPRESS, INC.—ASSESSING SPORT SPONSORSHIP EFFECTIVENESS

Richard L. Irwin, University of Memphis

• •

Over the past 20 years National Express, Inc., has established a strong reputation as a leader in the express shipping business. As the second largest shipper nationwide National Express, based in Newport, Tennessee, is always seeking means for improving market share and challenging their competition.

Disappointed at the company's inability to overtake their leading competitor, Allied Parcel Company, David Stone, founder and owner of National Express, replaced a majority of the executive staff including Tae-Ho Chin, Director of Sport & Event Marketing. Tae-Ho was a very likable man with great staff rapport. Not one person had ever been replaced within the unit since he assumed the position of director in 1985. The staff were very comfortable with him, and the unit was actively involved in a variety of sport events ranging from local youth leagues to sponsorship of "The National," a premiere event on the Professional Golf Association (PGA) Tour. However, in David's mind, Tae-Ho had failed to keep up with the times yielding the unit complacent. Make no mistake about it: The severance package offered to Tae-Ho provided for a comfortable retirement with 3 years' pay on top of the company retirement plan as well as bonus stock options.

Unfortunately, the department staff was leery of their new director, Jenny McDowell, who was recently hired from International Sports, Inc., a sport marketing agency in Phoenix, Arizona, where she spent 8 years assisting with several accounts including Coca-Cola's Olympic and National Football League sponsorships. Jenny had a wonderful reputation in the field and was seen as creative as well as articulate yet tough when needed. According to David, "she had it all." He was very confident that she was the right person for moving the department forward. The staff was pleased to hear that Jenny believed in laissez-faire management. Her philosophy was to assign, mentor when called upon, treat the staff in a mature manner, and evaluate.

Under Jenny's direction were five staff members, three men and two women, all of whom had been with the company for at least 8 years. They were a collegial bunch who spent a lot of their free time together. They all seemed to think alike and were considered great "PR types."

Within her first week on the job, Jenny called a staff meeting and requested that over the next 12 months a thorough assessment of each sponsorship activity be initiated with documentation supplied supporting the sponsorship investment. As she put it, the unit was spending in excess of $30 million dollars annually with little evidence of return on investment. Actually the directive was coming from David, who had grown frustrated with what he thought was frivolous spending within the Sport & Event Marketing unit. Although he, as much or more than anyone else, enjoyed attending the numerous events sponsored by National Express, he had grown concerned about the value obtained from each. Jenny challenged each staff member to design a sponsorship assessment protocol that would yield quantitative results that could be reviewed by all interested parties at sponsorship renewal time. At the conclusion she distributed some materials for the staff to review and offered a reminder that each sponsorship activity was intended to generate business for the company.

Oscar Montoya had been a staff member within National's Sport & Event Marketing unit for 10 years. A native of Newport, Oscar had volunteered to assist with The National every year since his senior year at Newport High. Upon completion of his undergraduate degree (B.A. in marketing) at Western Tennessee University, Oscar was hired by National as department representative. In his 10 years in that capacity, the tournament had experienced phenomenal growth. Annually record numbers were in attendance, television ratings were up, and leading tour money winners consistently participated. Oscar left the meeting certain these evaluation materials would not be all that difficult, but he only had 2 months to prepare. He also viewed this as a critical project as the event title sponsorship agreement was up for renewal. Because his job was directly linked to this specific event, it was imperative that he generate and forward favorable information.

Within a week Oscar did what all brilliant marketers would do: He called his former professor at Western Tennessee University and requested to meet with some students who might like to help with a research project. He wanted to employ two methodologies for collecting the quantitative-type data requested by Jenny. He proposed that one small group of students tape record the telecast of the event and calculate the total on-air exposure time received by National Express. This included in-focus viewing of coarse signage, pin flags, tee boxes, and National Express on-screen logo burn-ins, as well as oral mentions of National Express by the broadcasters. The second group was to execute exit interviews of event patrons simply seeking to know who they thought was the title sponsor of the event and the sponsors' business. To Oscar's delight, 15 students volunteered to assist with the event research.

As the title sponsor, National Express receives 1,000 tickets to the event as well as a provision to host a hospitality tent along the 18th fairway. Each year that Oscar had been associated with The National, all tickets had been distributed with many going to employees and the remainder to sales staff, and the hospitality tent, at an additional cost of $250,000 for catering, was always packed. With their share of the tickets, sales staff were encouraged to invite customers who they felt were deserving. Meanwhile, management typically invited 100 customers from across the country who spent more than $100,000 in shipping within the past year.

As the event approached, Oscar felt he had assembled a solid assessment of the event. His research crew was ready, all tickets had been distributed, no cancellations had occurred, and the television ad spots were set. Now if only Mother Nature would cooperate!

The event was a beauty. Jose Galdez birdied the final six holes to capture the lead from Chin Wei, who had led from the start. The fantastic charge by Galdez led to an impromptu plunge in the lake on Hole #18, which provided an ideal photo opportunity generating excitement among guests as well as extra exposure on sports pages and highlight shows all across the country. Jenny had attended and upon departure congratulated Oscar for providing a great hospitality environment. She demonstrated genuine enthusiasm for his report.

Now for Oscar's assessment responsibilities. As previously noted, all tickets had been successfully distributed and were in fact used for admission to the event. Overall attendance was up a record 13% with television ratings holding steady with the past 2 years.

Oscar chose to present a scrapbook-style bound copy of his findings to Jenny. He divided the results into the following sections: (a) attendance, (b) television, (c) additional media, (d) invited guests, and (e) general atmosphere. To his credit, Oscar believed he had compiled some rather convincing data that he provided in the report summary as follows:

- The on-site research revealed that 88% of the sample (N=1,000) correctly cited National Express as the title sponsor and 65% were familiar with their business category.
- Stabilized television ratings (3.1 with an 8 share) for the Saturday and Sunday rounds.
- Over 15 minutes (15:14) in on-air exposure time representing more than $3 million in commercial air time ($200, 000 per minute ad rate).
- Selected photos from national publications (e.g., *Sports Illustrated*, *Golf*, & *USA Today*).

- A comprehensive list of all invited guests who attended and their shipping performance over the past year.
- Photographs of the hospitality tent.

Within 21 days after the event's conclusion, Oscar submitted his report to Jenny. He anxiously awaited her comments as he assisted Betty Bowers with her preparations for the upcoming trade show.

Upon arriving at the office 2 days later, Oscar turned on his computer which notified him that he had an e-mail message from Jenny. He hurriedly clicked to view the following message:

Interoffice Memo

TO: Oscar Montoya
FROM: Jenny McDowell, Director
            Sport & Event Marketing
RE: "The National" Sponsorship Assessment

Initially, allow me to commend you for your evaluative initiatives related to our sponsorship of The National. You have provided some valuable, insightful data from which we can all derive a sense of accomplishment. Unfortunately, you have failed to provide concrete data that demonstrate we have accomplished our primary sponsorship goal(s)/objectives(s) via this sport sponsorship agreement. Without such facts our association with this event may be in jeopardy. It is imperative that we meet to discuss this situation this morning. Please be sure to bring the Guide to National Express Sponsorship Activity (distributed at our first staff meeting) with you.

Discussion Questions

1. What information might Oscar be lacking in his report?
2. How would he generate the additional information necessary to assess the sponsorship effectiveness?
3. Where did the problems start?
4. What should Jenny have done differently?
5. If you were hired as Oscar's replacement, how would you complete this task?
6. What resources are necessary?
7. What information is still accessible?

Suggested Readings/Resources

Crompton, J. L. (1994). Benefits and risk associated with sponsorship of major events. *Festival Management & Event Tourism, 2*, 65–74.

IEG Newsletter

Mullin, B. J., Hardy, S., & Sutton, W. A. (1993). *Sport marketing.* Champaign, IL: Human Kinetics Publishers.

Schaaf, P. (1995). *Sports marketing.* Amherst, BY: Prometheus.

Sponsor's Report

Related Professional Organization of Interest

International Events Group (IEG)
640 North LaSalle, Suite 600
Chicago, IL 60610-3777
(800)334-4850
http://www.sponsorship.com

STARTING A SPORT MARKETING FIRM

Wayne Blann, Ithaca College

Background

A group of male and female African-American and Latino entrepreneurs identified what they believed to be an opportunity for establishing a sport marketing firm that could develop its own niche in the marketplace. The entrepreneurs recognized that predominantly white-owned and -managed sport marketing firms were currently serving African-American, Latino, and other ethnic minority athletes using traditional (white-oriented) marketing strategies. It was their perspective that these traditionally white-owned and -managed sport marketing firms gave little, if any, consideration to their clients' race and ethnic or cultural backgrounds in developing marketing strategies. A further concern of these entrepreneurs was their view that minority athletes were, in some cases, being misrepresented and, perhaps, even exploited by the traditional approaches used to promote athletes. The African-American and Latino entrepreneurs also recognized that promotional programs involving minority athletes most often benefited events, organizations, and businesses that were already well established and controlled or owned by the dominant financial (white) classes of people. This was viewed negatively by the entrepreneurs because they believed that successful and highly visible athletes, especially minority athletes, should be encouraged to take actions to help businesses and people in the communities from which they came.

The African-American and Latino entrepreneurs wanted to establish a sport marketing firm owned and managed primarily by African-American, Latino, and other ethnic minorities that would develop promotional programs based upon an understanding and appreciation of their clients' race and ethnic and cultural backgrounds and needs. The entrepreneurs were also committed to developing promotional programs for their clients that would help address the financial, social, and moral issues faced by their communities.

Developing a Proposal for a Sport Marketing Firm

The entrepreneurs recognized that a first step in establishing a sport marketing firm was to obtain adequate financial support to support recruiting clients and initiating programs to serve clients during the first 3 years of operation and also to ensure financial stability for the future. It was decided that in order to identify and attract corporate sponsors, the entrepreneurs needed to develop a marketing plan that would (a) establish a distinctive mission; (b) establish clear objectives derived from the mission; (c) identify strategies for recruiting clients; (d) develop unique marketing activities/programs that would best serve the clients and, by so doing, distinguish the firm and differentiate it from its competitors in the marketplace; and (e) develop sponsorship packages that would appeal to and benefit both traditional (white-owned) corporations and African-American, Latino, and ethnic minority-owned businesses.

Developing a Marketing Plan

The entrepreneurs decided to consult with sport marketing experts (e.g., you and your classmates) in developing a marketing plan. Listed below are some of the questions they wanted help with in developing a plan.

Questions for Study

1. What market research do you recommend be undertaken to obtain the best possible data to assess the merits of this idea and to develop a marketing plan? Who should be surveyed? What information should be collected? What factors/trends in the marketplace need to be considered when interpreting the data? What ethical and social responsibility concerns need to be considered?

2. What purposes do you believe should be set forth in the mission statement? Explain how each purpose demonstrates ethical actions or social responsibility on the part of the firm.

3. What objectives do you recommend be written to carry out the mission?

4. What marketing activities/programs do you recommend be implemented to serve specific targeted audiences? How will these activities/programs help achieve the marketing objectives and fulfill the mission?

5. What steps would you take to identify corporate sponsors for the various marketing activities/programs?

6. What kind of sponsorship packages would you develop to appeal to and benefit different types of corporations?

7. What other questions do you believe need to be examined in order to successfully implement a marketing plan?

Educational Purposes of the Starting-a-Sport Marketing Firm Case Study

1. To develop students' understanding of how a sport marketing plan is derived from the mission and objectives of an organization.

2. To develop students' understanding of how sport marketing plans are developed within a sociocultural context.

3. To develop students' understanding of multiculturalism issues in developing sport marketing strategies.

4. To develop students' critical thinking skills in identifying ethical and social responsibility issues that exist within the broader social context and that influence how sport marketing strategies are developed.

Suggested Readings

Blann, F.W. (1998). Sport marketing. In J. B. Parks., B. R. K. Zanger, & J. Quarterman (Eds.), *Contemporary sport management* (pp.171–184). Champaign, IL: Human Kinetics.

Covey, S. R. (1989). *The seven habits of highly effective people.* New York: Simon and Schuster.

DeSensi, J. T. (1994). Multiculturalism as an issue in sport management. *Journal of Sport Management, 8,* 63–74.

Grunig, J. E,. & White, R. (1992). Communication, public relations, and effective organizations. In J.E. Grunig (Ed.), *Excellence in public relations and communications management.* Hillsdale, NJ: Erlbaum.

McCarville, R. E., & Copeland, R. P. (1994). Understanding sport sponsorship through exchange theory. *Journal of Sport Management, 8,* 102–114.

Slack. T. (1997). *Understanding sport organizations: The application of organization theory.* Champaign, IL: Human Kinetics.

Related Professional Organizations

African-American Athletic Association

Association of Black Women in Higher Education

Black Coaches Association
P. O. Box 4040
Culver City, CA 90231-4040
http://www.bca.org

National Alliance for Black School Educators
National Association for the Advancement of Colored People
(410)521-4939
http://www.naacp.org

National Chicano Council for Higher Education
National Network of Hispanic Women
12021 Wilshire Boulevard, Suite 353
Los Angeles, CA 90025
(213)225-9895

The National Urban League
http://www.nul.org

CALL YOUR OWN GAME: TRZ SPORTS SERVICES, INC.

Jacquelyn Cuneen, Bowling Green State University

TRZ Communications Services, Inc. (incorporated in 1984 as TRZ Sports Services, Inc.) was founded in 1982 in Akron, Ohio, to assist colleges, professional teams, and other sport organizations with fund-raising, ticket-sales program development, computer installation and instruction, broadcast network development, special event management and promotion, and other marketing, advertising, and public relation activities. While framing TRZ's various marketing, promotional, and sales activities, founder and Chief Executive Officer Thomas Zawistowski continued to work on a vision to develop a cost-efficient distribution system designed to bring college athletics games of all kinds to those graduates, boosters, and parents who were too widely dispersed to be reached by traditional radio and television broadcasts (TRZ Sports Services, 1994b).

Zawistowski's solution was to broadcast games using telephone services (TRZ Sports Services, 1994b). By March 1990, TRZ had arranged to broadcast all 32 games of the National Invitation (basketball) Tournament using a Kansas City, Missouri, service bureau owned and operated by a national long-distance carrier. The venture was a marketing achievement but a technical and financial disaster. Satisfied that the right technology could make telephone broadcasting possible and profitable, Zawistowski set out to acquire exclusive rights to distribute audio portions of games using a pay-to-listen concept, and in fall 1990, TRZ was using a service bureau in Omaha, Nebraska, to broadcast games. The Omaha venture was a technical and marketing success, but financial aspects remained problematic due primarily to a telephone-carrier system architecture that constrained profit. TRZ needed a way to provide the broadcast service at a price customers would be willing to pay yet that would generate profit for TRZ.

In December 1991, TRZ acquired a $1,000,000 investment (in exchange for 20% interest in the corporation) that enabled the company to build a propriety technical platform to make telephone broadcasting economically sound by the start of the 1992 college football season. Despite limited advertising and promotion activities (resulting from diminished capital due to the technical developments), the company continued to grow as the first enterprise to use telephone broadcasting.

Easy Access to Every Game in Any Market

TRZ revolutionized sports programming availability when it began TEAMLINE, an electronic medium designed to serve a fragmented market (TRZ Sports Services, 1994i). With TEAMLINE, live, unedited, unfiltered coverage of any sports event can be sent to fans across the country. Using their personal, business, hotel, cellular or pay phones from anywhere in North America, listeners access games, coaches' shows, press conferences, awards banquets, meetings, fundraisers, executive committee meetings, college/university presidential addresses, and sports informational services. Callers outside of North America use international operators and a national long-distance carrier. TEAMLINE operates primarily by feeding off the switchboard of each team's flagship radio station, but it can also feed from an office phone line, audio coupler or portable radio.

College sports are TRZ's primary broadcast stake. Initially, most institutions provided only football and men's basketball games from their radio flagships, but currently lacrosse, field hockey, ice hockey, and other sports that are not usually broadcast nationally are available regularly on TEAM-LINE. In 1993, telephone broadcast sales of college football increased 14%, of college men's basketball increased 55%, coverage of college women's basketball expanded to 32 teams, and college men's baseball sales doubled (TRZ Sports Services, 1994a) from the previous year. In the 1993–94 college seasons, 20,000 separate, live sporting events were broadcast via TRZ telephone lines (TRZ Sports Services, 1994e).

TRZ Targets

Sports "fanatics" were first identified as the target for TEAMLINE. Fans were perceived as an audience that would not be alienated by periodic miscues or service obstructions during initial development (TRZ Sports Services, 1994e); thus, TRZ could test and refine TEAMLINE's technical, interface, billing, and administrative fundamentals. Zawistowski thought fans would use TEAMLINE for three predominant reasons: (a) vast selections of games not scheduled for TV or radio broadcast, (b) opportunities to hear home team announcers, and (c) timeliness. There were four primary markets identified (TRZ Sports Services, 1994e, 1994f):

1. Sports fans who do not have regular geographic access to broadcasts of their favorite teams' contests.
2. Traveling fans who may wish to follow their favorite teams' contests while on the road and/or users who may also use TEAMLINE to listen to events not regularly available to them on local stations.

3. Newspaper, radio, and television reporters who listen to postgame or other programming from distant cities and/or follow distant games of local, regional, or national importance.

4. Individuals who monitor game and/or players' conditions for various reasons.

TEAMLINE Audience

The majority of TEAMLINE callers are male (96%). Average age of callers is 39, but age demography is distributed fairly evenly. Callers' average income is $71,000 (TRZ Sports Services, Inc., 1994c, 1994j), and most callers are college graduates. TEAMLINE audience demographics are shown in Tables 1 (age and income) and 2 (education).

Table 1
Age and Income Demography of TEAMLINE Callers

Age	%	Income	%
40-49	24	Over $50,000	53
30-34	22	$35,000-$50,000	17
35-39	21	$20,000-$35,000	15
18-29	18	Under $20,000	5
Over 50	14		

Note. Adapted from *Connections Magazine Fact Sheet*, p. 1, and *TEAMLINE Caller Demographics and Information Sheet*, p. 1, by TRZ Sports Services, 1994. Copyright 1994 by TRZ Communications Services, Inc. Adapted with permission of author.

Table 2
Education Demography of TEAMLINE Callers

Education	%
College Graduate	54.3
Master's Degree	27.7
Doctorate	6.0
High School Graduate	12.0

Note. Adapted from *TEAMLINE* Caller Demographics and Information Sheet, p. 1, by TRZ Sports Services, 1994. Copyright 1994 by TRZ Communications Services, Inc. Adapted with permission of author.

Income and education statistics are skewed by TEAMLINE promotion characteristics. TEAMLINE is promoted by colleges and universities to their alumnae/i bases. Therefore, listeners are likely to be college graduates with above-average incomes.

TRZ is committed to move telephone broadcasting from a niche market to a mass consumer product. TRZ national survey data indicate that the market contains 71 million consumers, only one tenth of one percent (1/10%) of whom have heard of TRZ's services. A survey conducted for TRZ in 1991 (TRZ Sports Services, 1994e) indicated that sales of audio sports services can reach $100 million annually.

Product

Thousands of people have access to the games of their choice on TEAM-LINE. Games are accessed by calling an 800 number, choosing the event(s) they wish, and listening for as long as they desire. Some users access several games for a few minutes each day or night. TEAMLINE is easy to access; Table 3 shows the procedure that callers use to access the TEAMLINE.

Table 3
Accessing TEAMLINE

- The TEAMLINE 800 number is dialed from any telephone in North America.
- The caller is prompted to punch in a team's 4-digit access code and select the event of choice.
- The caller is prompted to punch in major credit information.
- The credit card is verified, and the caller is connected to the event in seconds.
- Listeners are charged by the minute a declining retroactive rate ranging from $.30 to $.50 per minute. Rates decrease as listening time increases.
- Charges cease when listeners disconnect by hanging up (listeners are charged by time, not event).

Note. Adapted from *Annual report to CoSIDA* membership, p. 5, by TRZ Sports Services, 1994. Copyright 1994 by TRZ Communications Services, Inc. Adapted with permission of author.

Speaker phones and other add-on devices enable users to listen to TEAMLINE broadcasts just as they listen to radio broadcasts. Currently, TRZ holds exclusive pay-to-listen audio-transmission rights agreements with nearly 200 NCAA member schools (1994d). Teams from each major conference such as the Atlantic Coast, Big East, Big Eight, Big Ten, IVY, and Pacific-10, are included on TEAMLINE broadcasts (TRZ Sports Services, 1994o). TRZ also offers access to 28 National Football League teams, 26 teams in the National Hockey League, nearly half of all Major League Baseball, and several minor league baseball teams (TRZ Sports Services, 1994b, 1994e). Customers may call the same game as often as they like and may call different games on the same day or night. There is no set-up fee or minimum length for calls. College football games are the most frequently accessed (see Table 4); however TEAMLINE sales are dependent on the amount of advertising and promotion originated by the college/university, league/conference, and/or team.

Table 4
Sales for TEAMLINE Broadcasts

Sport	% of Caller Requests for Sport
College Football	46.8
NFL Football	21.4
NHL Hockey	21.0
College Basketball	10.8

Note: The information in this table is from *Connections* magazine fact sheet, (Page 1) by TRZ Sports Services, 1994. Akron, OH: TRZ Communications Services, Inc. Copyright 1994 by TRZ Communications Services, Inc. Adapted by permission.

That is, Table 4 shows that college football is the most frequently accessed sport. If colleges and universities promote TEAMLINE college football broadcasts heavily, then TEAMLINE's sales of college football rise; if TEAMLINE's service is not promoted, then sales fall. In other words, if colleges/universities promoted women's or men's basketball heavily, then those sports could supplant football as the most frequently accessed sport.

TRZ holds 1- to 3-year contracts with teams giving exclusive rights to distribute audio services on a pay-to-listen or subscription basis (TRZ Sports Services, 1994e). TRZ is negotiating currently with the National Basketball Association in order to provide scheduled NBA games to callers (TRZ Sports Services, 1994g). Table 5 shows the current status of contracts with TRZ collegiate and professional affiliates.

TRZ has an agreement with another communications and another sports marketing enterprise whereby TEAMLINE callers may order programs

Table 5
Current Status of TRZ Broadcast Contracts

Sport	Contract Terms in Years
Individual Colleges/Universities	3
NFL Football	1
NHL Hockey	2
College Basketball	3
All contracts contain first rights of renewal.	

Note. Adapted from *TEAMLINE Caller Demographics and Information Sheet*, p. 1, by TRZ Sports Services, 1994. Copyright 1994 by TRZ Communications Services, Inc. Adapted with permission of author.

and/or videos from the games they accessed and other events broadcast on TEAMLINE. Merchandise is mailed to customers after the game. Costs are dependent on market value (TRZ Sports Services, 1994a).

Incentives for Teams to Cooperate with TRZ

TRZ's major market goal is to have colleges and universities expand their uses of TEAMLINE by including more broadcasts of their nonrevenue sports, coaches' shows, press conferences, media days, team fundraisers, and other athletics functions (TRZ Sports Services, 1994g). TEAMLINE broadcasts offer sport enterprises several commercial benefits (see Table 6).

TRZ pays affiliates 12% gross of all revenue collected from sales of their events and 15% gross of revenues collected from third-party distributors. When events are offered in multiteam packages, TRZ allocates and distributes payments according to a formula developed by TRZ and the affiliates. Fee payments are made quarterly in December, March, June, and September.

TRZ proposes that TEAMLINE also benefits colleges and universities as a recruitment, retention, and endowment tool (TRZ Sports Services, Inc., 1994l):

1. Recruitment: Because even smaller schools can provide live coverage of any event, local fans, parents, and friends of players can hear every game. Local sports reporters have access to instant information relative to former high school players' performances, so local coverage is easy to disseminate. Institutions have found these elements to

Table 6
TEAMLINE's Benefits to Collegiate Athletics Departments

- TEAMLINE provides national and international access for fans who live beyond an institution's normal critical broadcast radius.

- Institutions receive commissions from TEAMLINE when any revenue is generated as a result of customers ordering their athletics programs events. Institutions receive a percentage of every dollar generated from calls to their events.

- Institutions can reach alumnae/i, fans and media nationally with game broadcasts, voice mail, fax or call transfers.

- Athletics programs receive national exposure for all sports.

- Players' families and the institutions' recruits have access to all live games.

- TRZ fund-raising activities related to long-distance calling are possible for institutions.

Note. The information in this table is from *Annual report to CoSIDA* membership, p. 4, by TRZ Sports Services, 1994. Copyright 1994 by TRZ Communications Services, Inc. Adapted with permission of author.

be important in recruiting athletes to their programs.

2. Retention: Players feel good about their college playing experiences when they know that their parents, friends, and former coaches can listen to their games. TEAMLINE also helps athletes' retention rates because the service can provide live coverage of classes that athletes miss while traveling.

3. Endowment: Colleges and universities have found that graduates respond to financial development needs when they are aware of them. Broadcasts of coaches' shows and live broadcasts of games help endowments by disseminating information relative to program needs.

TRZ Communications Services, Inc. also maintains voice-mail boxes and fax mailboxes, and provides call transfers for affiliated athletics programs. Rate charges for voice-mailboxes are flat fees of $4.95 per call for 5-minute updates. Fax mailboxes cost $2.95 for the first page and 99¢ for each additional page accessed from the mailbox. Users determine the limits for the number of pages contained in the fax boxes (TRZ Sports Services, 1994o).

Fund-Raising Programs

TRZ has continued its active involvement in fund-raising for college and university athletics departments by providing revenue ideas related to communication venues. A current project makes it possible for additional revenue to be generated through already existing donors when donors use

TRZ-issued telephone calling cards for regular long-distance calls (an independent long-distance carrier cooperates on the project). Portions of monthly payments (5% of a customer's collected long-distance dollar amounts) are allocated directly to a customer-designated athletics department. Athletics departments receive the monthly contributions at no extra cost to supporters; subscribers receive special long distance rates far below regular calling card rates (TRZ Sports Services, 1994h, 1994m).

TRZ and the carrier also offer a TEAMLINE debit calling card for travel or business use. The debit card is a prepaid calling card; when funds are depleted, cards are reloaded for the appropriate amount. Subscribers pay an average $.25 per minute with no access, connection, or monthly fees. Costs are approximately 40% less than regular calling cards; users receive a 5% rebate on every dollar of use to support their athletic programs (TRZ Sports Services, 1994a, 1994p).

TRZ Product Concepts for the Future:
Worldwide Audio and Video Access

TRZ's major action priority is to seek capital and recruit management talent to increase the scope and capacity of audio sports services (and also move toward nonsports interactive audio). TRZ would like to expand capacity by creating access points worldwide using the information superhighway. Projections show that interactive features and customization options would cut current unit costs 75% (TRZ Sports Services, 1994e). Current TRZ capital has been earmarked to purchase and install prototype hardware and software in major U. S. and Canadian markets. Increased cash flow is needed to help TRZ offset initial operating deficits for up to 18 months in each market. Portions of capital and profits will be used to establish and support national and local sales/marketing efforts.

TRZ' s current technology is able to deliver the audio portion of an unlimited number of live or time-delayed events to any home or business that has access to conventional telephone service and equipment. Only audio and low-to-moderate speed databases can be carried on public switchboard telephone networks (TRZ Sports Communications, 1994e); TRZ is investigating new call processing and bridging that will be capable of interfacing with video and foresees technology that can deliver black- and -white video signals over traditional analog telephone networks. Several manufacturers are developing low-cost customer-premise transceivers that would favor implementation of the system. TRZ research (TRZ Sports Services, 1994e) indicates that current customers are willing to pay up-front for the possibility of expediting black-and-white transceiver availability. Fiber optics can support cable TV, computer connections, and home management systems. When fiber-optic telephone lines become more common, TEAMLINE will be able to provide immense numbers of video events inexpensively.

TRZ projections show that black-and-white video service deployed over telephone lines would require a $1,500,000 investment. Engineering and development costs would use one half to two thirds of the capital for (a) designing and constructing prototype transceivers; (b) identifying, evaluating and selecting a manufacturer; and (c) covering unexpected cost overruns and initial promotional efforts.

Financial projections based on TRZ estimations of sales in new local and nonsports markets show that each expansion of network capacity and capability will require minimum incremental hardware and software investments of $25,000. Reaching each of the 50 largest North American markets would require capitalization of $1,250,000. Primary financing would be secured from cash flow generated by increased sales; overall income would be depressed initially due to operating shortfalls (TRZ Sports Services, 1994e).

Place

TEAMLINE games are delivered via radio broadcast or other audio signals using telephone, cable-television facilities, direct satellite, cellular technology and other electronic transmission methods serving homes, businesses, hotels, mobile phone units, and other locations. Home teams provide TRZ with phone lines for audio access. Broadcast teams are the home-site announcers.

The most recent market research (TRZ Sports Services, 1994c, 1994k) shows that 270,190 calls were placed to TEAMLINE in 1992; total minutes of use were 3,459,097. Average length of a call was 38 minutes with the longest single call lasting 270 minutes (4.5 hours). Reuse rate of first-time callers was 90%. Calls from the longest distance were placed from London, England (to hear California vs. Stanford football, December 17, 1990), and Johannesburg, South Africa (to hear Virginia Tech vs. Georgia Tech football on December 3, 1990).

TRZ has joined with an Atlanta company to provide TEAMLINE through cable telecasts beginning in Fall, 1994. Converters enable the TEAMLINE audio to be played through stereo systems. Test markets are Akron, Orlando, Spokane, and Roanoke. Cable prices begin at $5.00 per game ($19.95 per month); the monthly fee also includes access to 30 Music Choice channels. TRZ plans to expand the cable service nationwide by 1995 (TRZ Sports Services, 1994a).

Promotion

TEAMLINE's primary marketing method has been through joint advertising agreements with the teams (TRZ Sports Services, 1994e). Teams agree to promote TRZ services to fans, alumnae/i, and media through their press releases, game programs, media guides, local news features, booster magazines, arena/stadium signage, announcements in game broadcasts, public-address announcements, scoreboard messages, and so forth. TRZ provides free pictures, negatives, copy, camera-ready artwork for half- or quarter-page advertisements, broadcast quality audio- or videotape, and other materials to use in their promotions. College teams print advertisements at no charge for TRZ. TRZ also has rights to use teams' names, nicknames, and logos in national advertising.

TRZ has also used cooperative and per inquiry advertising with regional sports magazines linked to colleges and universities. The company has been satisfied with response to ads and plans to increase opportunities for cooperative advertising.

TRZ's Publication: Connections Magazine

TEAMLINE *Connections* is a monthly publication that contains daily programming guides, access codes for games, collegiate and professional rankings, news stories, and other features relative to sports teams and TEAMLINE programs. *Connections* is available by subscription for $2.50 per month.

Advertising is accepted in *Connections*. Advertising rates begin at $500 (see Table 7).

Table 7
Advertising Rates for CONNECTIONS Magazine

Full Page	Inside Front	Inside Back	Back	Center Spread
$500	$750	$750	$1,000	$1,000

Circulation: 50,000   Readership: 150,000 per issue
Rates are for page size of 5" x 7.5".

Note. Adapted from *Connections Magazine Fact Sheet*, p. 1, by TRZ Sports Services, 1994. Copyright 1994 by TRZ Communications Services, Inc. Adapted with permission of author.

The majority of *Connections* subscribers are from California, New York, and Florida (see Table 8), although *Connections* reaches subscribers in each state and the District of Columbia in some frequency.

Table 8
Geographic Distribution of CONNECTIONS Magazine Users

State	% Users	State	% Users	State	% Users
California	13.3	Alabama	2.0	D. C.	.6
New York	7.2	Maryland	1.9	Oklahoma	.5
Florida	6.9	Washington	1.9	Utah	.5
Illinois	4.6	Missouri	1.7	Nevada	.5
Texas	4.4	Arizona	1.3	Arkansas	.4
Virginia	4.4	Wisconsin	1.2	Nebraska	.4
North Carolina	4.1	Oregon	1.2	Alaska	.4
New Jersey	4.0	Colorado	1.1	New Mexico	.4
Georgia	3.8	Iowa	1.1	Delaware	.4
Ohio	3.5	Kentucky	.9	Idaho	.3
Pennsylvania	3.1	Louisiana	.8	Maine	.3
Tennessee	2.8	Kansas	.7	South Dakota	.3
Massachusetts	2.7	Minnesota	.7	Vermont	.3
Michigan	2.5	West Virginia	.7	Rhode Island	.2
Connecticut	2.5	New Hampshire	.7	Wyoming	.2
Indiana	2.2	Hawaii	.6	Montana	.2
South Carolina	2.1	Mississippi	.6	North Dakota	.1

Note. Adapted from *Connections Magazine Fact Sheet*, p. 1, by TRZ Sports Services, 1994. Copyright 1994 by TRZ Communications Services, Inc. Adapted with permission of author.

Some TEAMLINE affiliates in Ohio, Michigan, and Florida are test schools for a TEAMLINE Season Ticket and Business Boosters fund-raiser. Schools encourage their season ticket holders to use a TRZ company as their long-distance carrier; TRZ then charges the lowest possible long distance rate, and the schools receive monthly commissions from TRZ (commission is based on each dollar spent by holders on long distance). The program generates up to $25,000 per year for institutions.

Promotions for TRZ Fund Raising

TRZ markets their long-distance discount cards using brochures, advertisements in *Connections*, and target mailings. Athletics departments promote the cards to fans, boosters, and students through media of their choice (usually alumnae/i publications, game programs, mailings to boosters, and so forth). TRZ creates, funds and provides brochures to institutions, which distribute them to staff, season-ticket holders, donors, area boosters, and other supporters. Sign-up sheets are available in the brochures, or interested customers call an 800 number to subscribe. TRZ and the long-distance carrier complete the steps for telephone service and bill the customer monthly (TRZ Sports Services, 1994n).

Corporate Sponsorship

Sponsorship opportunities are available for corporations that wish to reach TEAMLINE customers (TRZ Sports Services, 1994p). Billboard commercials (such as "Today's game is brought to you by . . .") are available for each game, coaches' show, or team information line. Logo and theme line tags are also available in game program advertising, newspaper and magazine ads, merchandise, and other promotional items as well as in *Connections* (see Table 7).

Price

TEAMLINE users listen as long as they want from pre- to postgame (TRZ Sports Services, 1994i). Calls are timed from connection to disconnection. Discounts are given for each minute that callers stay on-line. Greatest rate card charge is 50¢ per minute; least charge is 20¢ per minute. A sample TEAMLINE rate card is shown in Table 9.

Average cost for users is 32¢ per minute. Canadian charges are higher due to higher costs of delivering the service, and all applicable charges apply to international calls (TEAMLINE *Connections*, 1994). Users are charged by their credit-card companies; TRZ pays the phone charges for each call and also pays 12% of each dollar generated to those affiliates whose fans call the events.

Initially, TRZ assessed a service charge of 50¢ for each call. Beginning in 1991, a $2.95 set-up fee was charged to cover initial cost, encourage longer calls, and eliminate short calls. When TRZ developed its own technology to access game feeds in 1992, set-up charges were dropped (TRZ Sports Services, 1994n).

Callers who used TEAMLINE beyond a 30¢-per-minute mark during

Table 9
Example Rates for TEAMLINE Broadcast

Minutes	Cost per Minute	Total Cost	Discount
1	$0.50	$ 0.50	- - -
15	$0.47	$ 7.06	6%
30	$0.44	$13.17	12%
45	$0.41	$18.34	18%
60	$0.38	$22.57	25%
75	$0.34	$25.85	31%
90	$0.31	$28.18	37%
105	$0.28	$29.57	44%
120	$0.25	$30.01	50%
135	$0.24	$32.14	52%
150	$0.23	$33.81	55%
165	$0.21	$35.10	57%
180	$0.20	$36.00	60%

Note. Adapted from *Connections*, p. 19, by TRZ Sports Services, 1994. Copyright 1994 by TRZ Communications Services, Inc. Adapted with permission of author.

the previous year and users who do not wish to use major credit cards when accessing games are encouraged to purchase a TEAMLINE season ticket (TRZ Sports Services, 1994i). Season tickets permit users to pay for phone charges in advance and save 25% or more per minute (cost of season-ticket minutes are as low as $.25). TEAMLINE Season Tickets are available at the start of each season. Season tickets are available in two packages (TRZ Sports Services, 1994k):

1. The Gold Season Ticket — a 900-minute credit for $225 (average cost per minute = 25¢).
2. The Silver Season Ticket — a 300-minute credit for $95 (average cost per minute = 32¢).

Users who have purchased season tickets find that hook-ups to games are faster because they only have to enter a 6-digit PIN number and, the team's 4-digit access code and select the event of their choice. Time to access games and events using a 20-digit credit card number and expiration date takes 50% longer. TRZ finds that customers are more likely to use prepaid cards over credit cards because the minutes have already been purchased. Trend examination shows that prepaid minutes are used despite overall season record or the significance of an individual game. Affiliates receive a negotiated percentage of each dollar generated by season-ticket usage.

The Price Incurred by TRZ

TEAMLINE's major costs in delivering games to customers are the long-distance charges incurred by bringing games over the phone lines to Akron, then bridging the call to the customer's phone. Projections show that by sending TEAMLINE directly to customers' local calling areas, TRZ would pay charges for one rather than two calls. TRZ is currently testing local access technology in the Cleveland market. Results will indicate the likelihood of providing local access to 50 cities to meet TRZ's goal of providing local access to 51% of the U. S. population.

TRZ Nonsport Product Interests

Technology proven to be sound by TEAMLINE's success has prompted TRZ to identify viable markets for other interactive audio services (TRZ Sports Services, 1994g).

Business programs: Providing live coverage of company press conferences, product announcements, and so forth for industry analysts, stockholders, and employees. Sales meetings and various restricted announcements could be narrowcast to those who hold security codes, such as institutional investors and vendors.

Entertainment: Providing coverage of daytime or nighttime programming, studio announcements, interviews, concerts, and tape-delayed broadcasts of commercial media programs for those who may have missed them when regularly scheduled.

Science: Providing coverage of presentations at major scientific conventions and announcements from major science centers and agencies.

Medicine: Providing 24-hour billing information to patients, eligibility requirements for state health-care assistance, and so forth with switching mechanisms so callers can code-in for live operators. TRZ is offering this service currently to a health-care corporation in Cleveland.

TRZ also foresees calling access for (a) conferences, (b) education programs, (c) customer and vendor information services, (d) various communications and database services, (e) news programs, (f) foreign language programs, (g) religion programs, (h) business programs, and (i) political programs. TRZ is certified by the Association of Professional Associations to deliver live or prerecorded continuing education events and to administer tests and validate identity of test subjects by using TRZ's interactive voice-response capabilities.

Note: The preceding case as written deliberately contains some information that is directly related to marketing problem solving and some information that may be irrelevant and/or unrelated. Readers must glean appropriate data in order to successfully complete a case study; different types of information will be useful for different questions and/or solutions.

Study Questions

1. Are the four primary markets identified for TEAMLINE still currently valid? That is, should TRZ continue to serve the fragmented market? What other markets might be attracted to TEAMLINE (i.e., what does general trend analysis indicate about the types of individualized, tailored services offered by companies such as TRZ)?

2. Does TEAMLINE really have any direct competition? That is, if fans have a chance to hear their favorite team's games anytime, even if network broadcasting is not carrying the games, what factors would keep them from listening?

3. How can TRZ convince customers that costs of telephone broadcasting are not prohibitive? What should be the focus of a TEAMLINE national promotional campaign in order to attract 51% of the U. S. population?

4. Typical demography for TEAMLINE callers shows that upscale ($71,000 income), 39-year-old, college educated males are TEAMLINE's primary users. What advertising, promotional, and public relations vehicles should TRZ use to attract more callers and enable TEAMLINE to attract the mass market?

5. In what ways should colleges and universities support use of TEAMLINE by their publics? How should colleges and universities promote TEAMLINE to their graduates, fans, boosters, and so forth? How could TRZ encourage colleges and universities to better promote TEAMLINE yet still maintain TRZ profits?

6. How can TRZ meet a major market goal to have colleges and universities provide TEAMLINE access to nonrevenue sports? Who are typical supporters of nonrevenue college and university sports? Should TRZ consider alternative pricing and profit-sharing strategies to encourage colleges and universities to offer more nonrevenue contests via TEAMLINE? Why would this be a sound or unsound strategy?

7. How could TRZ determine the size and scope of the market for listeners

of coaches' shows, press conferences, media days, team fund-raisers, and other functions?

8. TEAMLINE enjoys an exceptional reuse rate. Explain the market advantages of retaining customers. Identify ways in which TRZ could encourage reusers to place calls to TEAMLINE more often.

9. In what ways could TRZ convince numerous public service locations (such as hotels, restaurants/grills/bars, hospitals, and so forth) to promote TEAMLINE in their own advertising or promotional ventures? Design a profit-sharing plan for the location (i.e., teams receive 12% return; consider the percentage that would be justified for TRZ to pay a bar for broadcasting a game, yet would still enable TRZ to clearly make a profit.). Determine if such a market would be sizable enough for TRZ to offer some of its regular long-distance calling discounts to hotel, restaurant, or hospital management. How would TEAMLINE's demographics change if publics other than college/university graduates knew more about TEAMLINE? What advantages are there to a wide demographic base?

10. What advantages does TRZ's future market position (low cost black-and -white transceivers) lend to its current market position? That is, how does TRZ's current and future technological superiority reinforce current market position and dominate future position? How can TRZ use that position in its promotion of TEAMLINE?

11. How can TRZ start market planning in order to recoup the capital investments that will be spent to expand its coverage to video (i. e., how can TEAMLINE make profits and replenish investments from its offset)? What strategies should TRZ use currently to attract a large audience of TEAMLINE video users in the future?

12. In what ways could professional sport support use of TEAMLINE by their publics? How should professional sport promote TEAMLINE to their fans? How could TRZ encourage professional sport to promote TEAMLINE yet still maintain profits?

13. Design strategies by which TEAMLINE Gold or Silver Season Tickets could be promoted better by both colleges/universities and professional sports. What additional incentives could TRZ offer to colleges and universities in exchange for their heightened support?

14. In what ways could *Connections* magazine be used to better promote both TEAMLINE and itself? How could colleges/universities and professional sport alert fans to *Connections*? (Remember that most of *Connections* pages contain program schedules and access codes, but news,

rankings and other stories of interest are also featured.)

15. What states should TRZ target for intense promotional campaigns for TEAMLINE? (See Table 8; assume that *Connections* subscribers and TEAMLINE users are the same customers.) Is it more advantageous to target higher use areas, such as California, New York and Florida, or should TRZ concentrate on lower use areas, such as North Dakota, Montana, and Wyoming? Why? What rationale should determine targets?

16. Considering the overall demographics of TEAMLINE users and *Connections* readers, what enterprises (sport and nonsport) should be interested in using *Connections* as an advertising vehicle?

17. What strategies can TRZ use to convince corporations that sponsorships of broadcasts can reap both monetary and public relations advantages? What pricing structure should apply to sponsorships? Should pricing be based on past frequency of calls for certain teams, or should TRZ's sponsorship rate be based on preseason standings? That is, should the price of sponsoring games featuring Division I football bowl contenders be more expensive than sponsoring games that have proven to be popular yet are "insignificant" in national standings (i.e., should pricing be based on the game, or the number of callers)?

18. How can TRZ encourage college and universities to use the fund-raising components of both TRZ and TEAMLINE? What other TEAMLINE-related fund-raising strategies could TRZ offer to colleges and universities?

19. How can TRZ's plans to enter nonsport-related telephone broadcasting (business, entertainment, science, medicine, and so forth) enhance their market position relative to sport? How can TRZ determine if combination packages (offering cards for exclusive sport and entertainment use, or sport and medicine use, and so forth) would be feasible?

20. Design a promotional strategy showing that costs of TEAMLINE game broadcasts are not prohibitive. That is, convince displaced collegiate and professional sports fans that the cost structure for TEAMLINE differs substantially from regular long-distance charges and suggest ways that fans could use TEAMLINE to follow their favorite games.

Suggested Readings

Balasubramanian, S. K., & Kamakura, W. A. (1989). Measuring consumer attitudes toward the marketplace with tailored interviews. *Journal of Marketing Research, 26,* 311–326.

Gordon, C. (1987, August). Taking a grassroots approach to research. *Marketing News*, 22.

Hofacre, S., & Burman, T. K. (1992). Demographic changes in the U. S. into the twenty-first century: Their impact on sport marketing. *Sport Marketing Quarterly, 1* (1), 31–36.

Park, C. W., Roth, M. S., & Jacques, P. F. (1988). Evaluating the effects of advertising and sales promotion campaigns. *Industrial Marketing Management, 17*, 129–140.

Peppers, D. & Rogers, M. (1993). *The one to one future: Building relationships one customer at a time.* New York: Doubleday.

Pitts, B. G., Fielding, L. W., & Miller, L. K. (1994). Industry segmentation theory and the sport industry: Developing a sport industry segmentation model. *Sport Marketing Quarterly. 3* (1), 15–24.

Pitts, B. G., & Stotlar, D. K. (1996). *Fundamentals of sport marketing.* Morgantown, WV: Fitness Information Technology, Inc.

Stier, W. F. (1992). Understanding fundraising in sport: The conceptual approach. *Sport Marketing Quarterly, 1* (1), 41–46.

Sutton, W. (1987). Developing an initial marketing plan for intercollegiate athletic programs. *Journal of Sport Management, 1*, 146–158.

References

TEAMLINE *Connections*. (1994, November). Akron, OH: TRZ Communications Services, Inc.

TRZ Sports Services. (1994a). *Annual report to CoSIDA membership*. Akron, OH: TRZ Communications Services, Inc.

TRZ Sports Services. (1994b). *Company history*. Akron, OH: TRZ Communications Services, Inc.

TRZ Sports Services. (1994c). *Connections magazine fact sheet*. Akron, OH: TRZ Communications Services, Inc.

TRZ Sports Services. (1994d). *Exclusive pay-to-listen audio transmission rights agreement*. Akron, OH: TRZ Communications Services, Inc.

TRZ Sports Services. (1994e). *Executive summary*. Akron, OH: TRZ Communications Services, Inc.

TRZ Sports Services. (1994f). *The four primary markets for TEAMLINE*. Akron, OH: TRZ Communications Services, Inc.

TRZ Sports Services. (1994g). *The future of TRZ communications services, Inc*. Akron, OH: TRZ Communications Services, Inc.

TRZ Sports Services. (1994h). *Go team*. Akron, OH: TRZ Communications Services, Inc.

TRZ Sports Services. (1994i). *How TEAMLINE works*. Akron, OH: TRZ Communications Services, Inc.

TRZ Sports Services. (1994j). *TEAMLINE caller demographics and information sheet*. Akron, OH: TRZ Communications Services, Inc.

TRZ Sports Services. (1994k). *The TEAMLINE season ticket*. Akron, OH: TRZ Communications Services, Inc.

TRZ Sports Services. (1994l). *Telephone broadcasting*. Akron, OH: TRZ Communications Services, Inc.

TRZ Sports Services. (1994m). *The TRZ/BN1 long distance fund raising program*. Akron, OH: TRZ Communications Services, Inc.

TRZ Sports Services. (1994n). *TRZ TEAMLINE rate card (past and present)*. Akron, OH: TRZ Communications Services, Inc.

TRZ Sports Services. (1994o). *What TEAMLINE has to offer to its corporate sponsor*. Akron, OH: TRZ Communications Services, Inc.

TRZ Sports Services. (1994p). *You make the call*. Akron, OH: TRZ Communications Services, Inc.

Related Professional Associations

National Association of Broadcasters
1771 N Street
Washington, DC 20036
Radio members phone: (800)455-5394 [in the U.S.], (202)429–5400
http://www.nab.org/

Acknowledgments

The author gratefully acknowledges Thomas Zawistowski, Chief Executive Officer, and Kim Snyder, Executive Assistant, TRZ Sports Services, for their valuable contributions to this project.

CATCH THAT CHAMPIONSHIP FEVER!!

Richard L. Irwin, University of Memphis

●●●

Introduction

Ernie English is experiencing one of those weeks that many of us only dream about. Having been recently hired as the Associate Athletic Director for Marketing and Promotions at a university that has qualified for the national championship football game Ernie is prepared to relish the team's recent accomplishments. Hey, it's events like this that typically improve booster donations, corporate sponsorship, and attendance—all responsibilities assigned to Ernie when he accepted this position a short time ago. Life couldn't be better for the rapidly ascending athletic administrator. However, Ernie, as well as his immediate predecessors, has failed to adequately address one critical element of the contemporary sport promotional mix: licensing. This is about to turn Ernie's dream week into a major nightmare.

Background

Ernie English was recently hired as the Associate Athletic Director for Marketing and Promotions at Western Tech in Commerce City, Colorado. Tech is a state-funded institution founded in 1898 with an enrollment of approximately 7,500 full-time students. Commerce City, on the other hand, is a "bedroom" community nestled at the base of the Rocky Mountains (or so it says in the school promotional literature!). A town of approximately 80,000 citizens, Commerce City has many residents who commute daily to work in Denver.

Ernie's official date of employment was December 1 due to an extended search to find the perfect person and the fact that his predecessor departed in the midst of fall sports in order to accept a position with the expansion Rocky Mountain Rockies of the newly formed United States Baseball Association (USBA). Ernie's position has been expanded to include a variety of marketing-related and revenue production-oriented tasks including event and team promotions, ticket sales, corporate sponsorship, booster club management, and licensing. Prior to accepting the Tech position, Ernie had served as the Athletic Marketing Assistant at South Central University, an NCAA Division II school in Broken Arrow, Oklahoma. His primary responsibilities at South Central were associated with team and event management as well as corporate sales. Ernie earned his master's degree in sport management from Midwestern University prior to accepting the position at South Central and after earning a bachelor of arts in business administration at Pacific Western.

His first few weeks on the job have been very exciting as the Western Tech "Techsters" have experienced the most unbelievable football season in school history. The team has advanced unscathed through the NCAA Division II Football Playoffs after finishing the regular season 12-2 and claiming the Mountain States Conference Championship. The Techsters' opponent in the national championship game will be Capitol College from Midland, Texas. Appearing in the title game is nothing new for the Capitol College Statesmen, who have dominated NCAA Division II Football the past 12 years winning eight championships as well as three runner-up trophies.

The Championship Fever

The campus as well as community has been abuzz as the Mighty Techsters have never before qualified for a national playoff, let alone the championship game, in any team sport. Attendance at the one home playoff game against Divinity College was 11,990 after averaging 8,562 during the regular season. Immediately following the semifinal victory over the Midland University Plainsmen this past Saturday, many local businesses began offering "Techster Specials" that ranged from free Techster logo cups with the purchase of a "full meal deal" at the four Bellybuster Cafes in Commerce City to no cover charge at Orville's Hangar, a local student hangout, for anyone wearing Techster logo apparel.

The Call

On the Monday prior to the championship game, slated to be played at the Georgia Dome in Atlanta, when Ernie returns from attending the weekly Techster Booster Club Meeting at the Buckboard Tavern, he has received calls from Angie Ehrhart, Director of Licensing at the NCAA, as well as Rusty Miller, National Sales Director for Specialty Sports of Tunica, Mississippi, the Official Concessionaire of the NCAA.

Each of the callers has requested permission for Ernie, on behalf of Western Tech, to grant Specialty Sports permission to use the WT logo on all championship merchandise to be sold at the championship game in Atlanta. Ernie chooses to return Angie's call first, and she informs him that the NCAA commonly enters into a three-way, short-term joint license agreement with participating institutions for all national championship events. This arrangement entitles all parties involved to share equally in the royalties generated from the sales and distribution of Specialty Sports merchandise. According to Angie, this arrangement has proven quite lucrative for participating institutions in the past with some schools generating several thousand dollars over the championship weekend. To expedite the process, Angie recommends that Ernie forward a short-term license agreement to her and Rusty indicating that the NCAA, Capitol, and Western will act as colicensors and designating Specialty Sports as the exclusive licensee of the arrangement.

This all sounds quite impressive to Ernie, particularly the ability to generate the much-needed revenue. However, when Ernie casually mentions to Angie that Western Tech does not currently have an official licensing program in operation, she expresses a sense of amazement. In fact, she erroneously tells him that this may terminate the possibility of royalty sharing. Although he later finds this not to be true, it does raise some immediate concern, and his stress level is beginning to rise.

Ernie concludes the conversation with Angie indicating that he will request the university legal affairs office draft a contract outlining the specific information needed to appropriately execute the agreement. She allows him until Wednesday to fax to her and Specialty Sports the completed contract. In the meantime he must forward Specialty Sports the Techster logo slicks and PMS colors for printing as well as a standards manual describing how the logos should be displayed.

Immediately following his conversation with Angie, Ernie calls the Office of Legal Affairs in hopes of getting some assistance with this situation. Unfortunately, the University Counsel is out until late in the afternoon. Ernie's next call is to the Office of Sports Information to see if they have a standards manual. Bert Bestgien, the Sports Information Director, who thinks that having a standards manual would be a great idea but has never seen one for Western Tech in his 24 years on campus, refers him to Printing Services. When Ernie reaches the receptionist in Printing Services she indicates that he must obtain the approval of Tim Baake, Printing Services Manager, before she can release an official copy of the standards manual. Unfortunately, Tim is also out of the office but will return at 8 a.m. Tuesday morning.

Finally, at approximately 3:30 p.m. Mountain Standard Time, Glen Gagnon, the university legal counsel, returns Ernie's call. After Ernie explains the problem, Glen indicates that it will not be difficult to draft a *modified* license agreement for the purposes described by Angie; however, he is leaving in the morning for a legal seminar in Santa Clara, California, and will not return until Sunday. He suggests that Ernie call Angie back immediately and ask if they have a copy of a contract that could modified by

Western Tech for this weekend's event. What a great idea! Ernie hangs up immediately and dials the NCAA Headquarters in Overland Park, Kansas, only to be reminded that they are on Central Standard Time and their offices have closed for the day. When Ernie attempts to call Glen, the receptionist relays that he has departed for the day.

Following a stroll to the soft drink machine for a dose of caffeine and a moment to collect his thoughts on this issue, Ernie returns to his office to find a message from Sally Lees, the women's gymnastics coach. When he contacts her, Sally says that she had been to the Student Center for lunch and observed some fraternity brothers distributing T-shirts prominently bearing the Techster athletic logo, which has always been a block-letter-style capital WT as displayed in Figure 1, along with the words *Kick Capitol's Ass*. Sally also said that when she confronted the young men, they indicated that they were selling the shirts as a fraternity fund-raiser. When asked if they had obtained permission to use the school's athletic logo the young men responded negatively and suggested that because they were full-tuition-paying students at the school, they should not need to request such permission. Lastly, one of the more rational young men asked Ms. Lees from whom such permission should have been obtained, and when she expressed uncertainty, her argument with them appeared to be rendered mute.

Figure 1

After listening to her description of the situation Ernie could not help but ask Sally why she has brought this information to him. Her response is "Isn't licensing a part of marketing and promotions? For heaven's sake, what were you hired to do, coordinate bake sales?"

Yes, in fact, Ernie had been told that licensing would eventually become a part of his job responsibilities within the athletic department. The key word was *eventually*. Unfortunately, licensing is not an area in which Ernie has been well trained. He remembers his sport management professor, Dr. Terry Davis, talked about licensing occasionally and indicated to the students that it was emerging as a major marketing and promotional issue as well as revenue source for sport organizations of all types. However, Ernie chose not to actively pursue the topic, a decision that is beginning to haunt him at this moment.

In concluding his conversation with Sally, Ernie requested the name of the involved fraternity. Sally says it was the Alpha Betas, a fraternity that is very supportive of all athletic teams and one that is attempting to organize a group to attend the title game in Atlanta.

Ernie decides to follow Sally's request and contact the AB House. Not sure of exactly what he is going to say, he gets the House answering machine that essentially verbalizes the message contained on the t-shirts for sale at the student center. Ernie leaves a message requesting a house representative contact him at their earliest convenience.

As the time approaches 5 p.m. Ernie remembers that he has set an appointment with Dirk Rosenbaugh, General Manager of Goldsby's Department Store. The meeting is to discuss a possible sponsorship for men's and women's Basketball. Goldsby's has always been a supporter of the athletic department as Dirk was a four-time letter winner in tennis while receiving a bachelor's degree in business administration.

Dirk's office is near the men's section in the store, but Ernie decides to enter through the children's section to see if he can get any Christmas ideas for his 8-year old niece, Samantha. As Ernie approaches the entrance, he notices a huge banner over the entry welcoming all Techster Fans to Goldsby's and wishing the Techsters Good Luck against the Statesmen. Just inside the door is an elaborate display of Techster logo merchandise. Items include T-shirts, sweatshirts, caps, pennants, posters, and windsocks. At first Ernie is overwhelmed with joy—these people really love the Techsters! Then he thinks that this is going to be an easy sell. Finally, as he comes to his senses, he begins to wonder if the school has approved the usage of their logo on any of this merchandise.

Ernie decides to bypass the shopping and head directly for Dirk's office. Along the way he finds several other Techster logo items ranging from seat cushions to writing pads. Because he is relatively new, he is not sure if this is common or due to the Techsters' trip to the national championship. He also begins to wonder who is producing and supplying all this stuff.

When Ernie arrives at Dirk's office, it too is decorated in the blue and gold of Western Tech. Dirk himself proudly wears a tie emblazoned with the Techster logo. Ernie chooses to stick with the issue at hand initially. He discusses with Dirk the potential categories of sponsorship and the various entitlements. Dirk is waffling and making things somewhat difficult. When it appears that Dirk is going to balk at a sponsorship, Ernie blurts out rather unprofessionally, "You either become a sponsor, or remove all the unlicensed merchandise from your store."

Dirk asks Ernie to clarify his comments and define "unlicensed merchandise." Ernie is a bit lost for words. He indicates, similar to Sally's confrontation with the fraternity brothers, that Dirk has not obtained permission to display Techster logo merchandise. Dirk states that he is not the producer of the goods, nor does he need any permission to display the merchandise because there is no existing policy that prohibits this action. Second, he contends that he asked the athletic director, Geri Weaver, on several occasions from whom he should order school logo merchandise and never received a response. Last, Dirk states that the school logos are public property and that all tax-paying citizens have the right to use them if they so wished. He adds that while studying business at Tech, he learned a lot about licensing and that he is well aware of his rights as a tax payer as well as business person.

Ernie asks Dirk whom he is in fact receiving the merchandise from, and Dirk says a variety of imprinting companies but declines to provide any specific information. Somewhat bewildered Ernie decides to conclude the meeting and asks Dirk if he can delay his final decision until after the football game. Dirk agrees and offers Ernie a Techster logo pen as a parting gift. Ernie is well aware that this is a jab from Dirk, who is well known for his arrogant stunts.

Just before leaving Ernie remembers that he needs to pick up an anniversary card for his parents. Because Goldsby's is the anchor store of the Commerce City Megamall, this is the most convenient time to stop at the card shop. Next door to Carl's Cards is The Jocque Shop, which has a full window display of Techster merchandise similar to that found at Goldsby's. Ernie decides to go undercover and obtain key inside information.

He enters the store and appears interested in the Techster merchandise hoping to attract the attention of a sales associate. Eventually, a teenage associate wanders over and offers to help Ernie if he needs it. Ernie expresses his interest in the Techster paraphernalia and asks the teenager if he knows where it was made. The teenager proudly responds, "Right in the back of the store! Isn't it way cool? Do you want to place a big order?" Ernie declines but asks if he could talk to the manager. The teenager sheepishly retrieves the manager from their office and points in the direction of Ernie.

Ernie introduces himself to Mr. Jocque LaBonde, store owner and general manager as well as former All-American ice hockey player for the Techsters during the early 1980s, who turned professional one semester shy of completing his undergraduate degree in marketing. Following a brief stint in the National Hockey League and International Hockey League, Jocque returned to Commerce City to work. He used his signing bonus to start The Jocque Shop, a very lucrative business that now includes franchises in seven Western region cities.

Ernie tells Jocque that he greatly appreciates his support of the school but feels that first permission should have been obtained before Jocque produced items bearing the logo of the school and that the school was entitled to recoup a portion of the revenues generated from this use. At this Jocque bursts into laughter and states, "I've been doing this for well over 10 years, and now you barge in here after the wimpy football team finally achieves a little success and demand that I start paying for this stuff! You must be joking."

Ernie informs Jocque that the wheels are in motion to develop new policies that will disallow unauthorized use of the school athletic logo for commercial purposes. Jocque, who stands 6'3" and looks as if he could still hold his own on the ice, does not appear too intimidated by Ernie's comments. In fact, he responds with, "If you come after me, are you going after the bookstore? Those are the people ripping everyone off!"

With that Ernie heads for home, forgetting about his parents 25th anniversary and his niece's Christmas interests. He is now on a mission.

When Ernie arrives at the office on Tuesday ready to address the situation, he immediately receives an intercampus package from Tim Baake in Printing Services. Inside the package is the standards manual he requested on Monday, a standards manual request form requiring the department head's signature to be returned to Mr. Baake, and a memo from Tim wishing the Techsters good luck this weekend. Ernie breathes a sigh of relief. This licensing stuff isn't going to be all that tough. A good standards manual demonstrating the proper logo presentation requirements, a few solid operational policies, and a hard-nosed approach are all that it is going to take.

Then he opens the manual and discovers it was designed for school stationery letterhead only and has not been updated since the athletic department added gold as an accent color in 1985. That's when the phone rings. On the other end is Angie Ehrhart from the NCAA inquiring about the status of the school standards manual and short-term joint-use license agreement.

Suggested Discussion Issues

Ernie is obviously confronted with a number of licensing-related issues. Please describe in detail how you recommend Ernie deal with the following in the short-term (prior to the championship football game):

- The NCAA & Specialty Sports
- Bellybusters
- The Alpha Betas
- Goldsby's
- The Jocque Shop
- The Bookstore

In your response, please be sure to thoroughly describe your suggested course of action and the rationale for these procedures. Essentially, what grounds does Ernie have for your recommended course of action? Is there any legal or ethical foundation? What consideration must be given to community public relations?

In the long term, do you think that the university should initiate a licensing program? Why or why not? If they should, how would you recommend that Ernie go about establishing such a program?

What type of licensing-program operational policies do you recommend for adoption? What departments on campus should be actively involved in the creation and execution of the licensing operational policies? Should any royalty exemptions be granted to internal or external organizations? How would you suggest Ernie deal with promotional licensing agreements?

Suggested Readings

Irwin, R. (1991). A license to profit. *College Athletic Management, 3* (1), 18–23.

Irwin, R. L., & Stotlar, D. K. (1993). Operational protocol analysis of sport and collegiate licensing programs. *Sport Marketing Quarterly, 2* (1), 7–16.

Irwin, R. L., Stotlar, D. K., & Mulrooney, A. L. (1993). A critical analysis of collegiate licensing policies and procedures. *The Journal of College and University Law, 20* (3), 97–109.

Merchandising Reporter
Team Licensing Business

Professional Associations

Association of Collegiate Licensing Administrators (ACLA)
The Collegiate Licensing Company (TCLC)
Attn. Bruce B. Siegel, Esq.
320 Interstate North, Suite 102
Atlanta, GA 30339
(770)956-0520

Licensing Resource Group (LRG)
426 Century Lane, Suite 100
Holland, MI 49423
(616)395-0676
http://www.lrgusa.com

Industry Segmentation Theory and the Sport Industry: Developing a Sport Industry Segment Model

THEORY

Brenda G. Pitts, Ed.D.
Lawrence W. Fielding, Ph.D.
Lori K. Miller, Ed.D.
University of Louisville

ABSTRACT

The purpose of this study was to apply industry segmentation theory to the sport industry and to develop a sport industry segment model. Porter's (1985) theory of industry segmentation was applied. Traditional and contemporary definitions of sport and sport industry as well as lists and descriptions of sport products were used. The results produced three sport industry segments: sport performance, sport production, and sport promotion. In addition, product variety categories and buyer types were identified in each segment.

Drs. Brenda Pitts, Lawrence Fielding, and Lori Miller are faculty members in the Sport Management Program at the University of Louisville.

In planning for competitive advantage, a bat-making firm decides to identify, define, and offer a new product designed specifically for a new target market--a youth market (Fielding, Pitts, & Miller, 1991). The decision is based on two areas of information: the consumer segment and the competition. The consumer segment, or target market, consists of those who are buyers or potential buyers of a product. The competition consists of those firms offering or potentially offering the same product or a substitute product to satisfy consumer need. Analysis of both is critical in the decision-making process for sport marketing strategies.

In the words of Porter (1985), "Competitive advantage is at the heart of a firm's performance in competitive markets" (p. xv). Competition shapes the firm's strategies and activities in its quest for a profitable and sustainable position in an industry (Porter, 1985). Further, Porter points out that industries are not homogeneous. There are various segments within any given industry. Segments differ in many ways, yet boundaries may fluctuate due to a multitude of factors, one of which is product substitutability.

In some cases of industry segmentation, segments are found to be so different that they are reclassified as an industry. The deciding factor, or boundary, may be interrelationships between segments. Where interrelationships between segments are strong, those segments may be considered as true segments of an industry. For example, all sport, recreation, leisure, and fitness activity products (activities for participation) serve to meet specific buyer needs or desires: fun, fitness, competition, entertainment. Where interrelationships between segments are weak, those segments may be considered separate industries. For example, one may argue that recreational soccer--a product offered for participation for beginners, intermediates, and a few advanced players--is so very different from professional soccer--a product offered for the participation of the elite player and primarily for spectating--that they may be considered separate industries. Indeed, many segments of the sport industry may be considered separate and complete industries with no interrelatedness to other segments. The marketing and/or management person must determine the answer to these boundary questions and decide how to position the firm toward gaining and sustaining competitive advantage.

Porter also elaborates that industry segmentation should go beyond accepted models of segmentation. Final decisions on segment boundaries are always a matter of degree. Industry segmentation should be considered a tool in guiding one toward industry structural analysis. Such analysis serves to expose key elements of competitive advantage (Porter, 1985).

> **In pursuit of contributing to the development of a body of knowledge in sport management, and specifically to sport marketing, as fields of study, we believe that academicians, students, and practitioners will benefit from a study of the sport industry through industry segmentation.**

"An industry is a market in which similar or closely related products are sold to buyers" (Porter, 1985, p.233). Some industries may contain just one product variety. It is more typical that an industry contains a variety of product items sold to many existing or potential consumers who vary demographically and psychographically, and who may change in need, want, or demand. Companies within an industry segment "create new product varieties that perform new functions, combine functions in new ways, or split off particular functions into separate products" (Porter, 1985, p. 233). Similarly, new consumers may become part of an industry, existing consumers may change their need, or consumers may drop out of an industry (Porter, 1985).

An industry segment is a combination of a product variety (or varieties) and a group of consumers who purchase it. Industry segmentation is the division of an industry into subunits for purposes of developing competitive strategy (Porter, 1985). The primary reason for industry segmentation is competitive strategy formulation. Other

reasons include to identify marketing opportunities and threats within a specific product market, to develop an appropriate marketing mix, and to inform major resource allocation decision making (Day, Shocker, & Srivastava, 1979; McCarthy & Perrault, 1990; Porter, 1985).

Although there is some research on defining and delineating the sport industry, we found no attempts to apply Porter's industry segmentation theory. Current research in defining, delineating, and segmenting the sport industry includes the following: (a) identifying consumer markets in various sports (see consumer marketing reports, such as American Sports Data, Inc., the Sporting Goods Manufacturers Association marketing reports, and the National Golf Foundation's marketing reports); (b) delineating the sport industry according to career segments (see Parks & Zanger, 1990); and (c) defining and delineating the industry according to type of sport setting (see, for example, DeSensi, Kelley, Blanton, & Beitel, 1990). Although the research on consumer markets and sport-setting types may be used by the sport marketer in competitive strategy formulation, the career-setting information is targeted for use by the student of sport management.

In pursuit of contributing to the development of a body of knowledge in sport management, and specifically to sport marketing, as fields of study, we believe that academicians, students, and practitioners will benefit from a study of the sport industry through industry segmentation. In particular, the research may be of value to instructors of courses in sport marketing, sport management, or of similar courses in competitive strategy, strategic planning, or strategic marketing planning and management.

The practitioner may use industry segmentation information to inform decisions concerning where to compete within an industry and where to focus company strategies within an industry; to identify opportunities and threats within an industry segment; to create new industry segments; or to inform decisions concerning exiting a segment. It was, therefore, the purpose of this research to apply Porter's (1985) industry segmentation theory to the sport industry.

The Porter Model
To segment an industry, four segmentation variables are used (for a complete discussion on industry segmentation, see Porter, 1985). Any one or any combination of the variables may be used. Porter's four segmentation variables are presented with a brief discussion of each.

1. **Product Segments:** The discrete product varieties that are, or could be, produced" (Porter, 1985, p.238). Product segments are developed by identifying all the product offerings produced or potentially produced within an industry. Defining characteristics may include physical size, price level, features, functions, technology or design, inputs employed, packaging, performance, new vs. aftermarket or replacement, product vs. ancillary services or equipment, and bundled vs. unbundled. Product de-

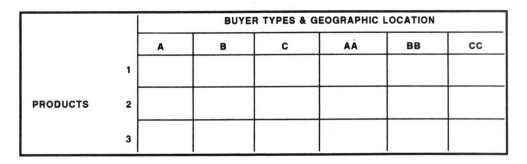

**Figure 1. A simple Industry Segmentation Matrix (top left and right)
and a Combined Matrix of three variables (bottom)**
(Adapted from Porter, 1985)

scriptors may be combined in a variety of ways to define a particular segment.

2. **Buyer Segments:** "The types of end buyers that purchase, or could purchase, the industry's products" (Porter, 1985, p. 238). Buyer, or market, segmentation always produces debate. Boundaries that might determine buyer differences and segments of buyers can differ from marketer to marketer and from company to company. Segmentation should reflect differences among buyers because the goal of segmentation is to expose all these differences. Porter divides buyers into two categories: industrial and commercial buyers and consumer goods buyers. Industrial and commercial buyers may be defined by the following: buyer industry, buyer's strategy, technological sophistication, equipment manufacturers vs. users, vertical integration, decision-making unit or purchasing process, size, ownership, financial strength, and order pattern. Consumer goods buyers may be defined using the following variables: demographics, psychographics or life-style, language, decision-making unit or purchasing process, and purchase occasion.

3. **Channel Segments:** "The alternative distribution channels employed or potentially employed to reach end buyers" (Porter, 1985, p. 238). Differences in channels may include direct vs. distributor, direct mail vs. retail or wholesale, distributors vs. brokers, types of distributors or

retailers, and exclusive vs. nonexclusive outlets.

4. **Geographic Segments:** "The geographic location of buyers, defined by locality, region, country, or group of countries" (Porter, 1985, p. 238). Geographic location variables affect product purchase decisions according to product attributes due to differences in weather, customs, government regulations, and other geographical differences. Some variables are localities, regions, or countries, weather zones, and stage of national development or other country groupings.

METHODOLOGY

A comprehensive industry analysis for segmentation requires the development of a matrix using all four segmentation variables and each category that is relevant (Porter, 1985). This may result in a matrix so large and complex that it becomes confusing, unmanageable, and most likely not useful. The task, then, is to aggregate variables into meaningful segments. Segmentation may be achieved using any one of the variables (product, buyer, channel, and geographic location). Some examples are shown in Figure 1.

Definition of Sport and Sport Industry

For our purposes in this research, we used definitions of sport and sport industry from Pitts (1988) and Pitts,

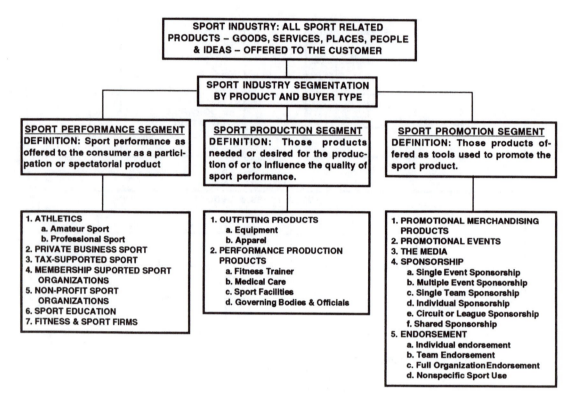

Figure 2. The Sport Industry Segment Model

Fielding, and Miller (1991). Although sport has been defined in many ways, it typically refers to physical activity through some form of organized and regulated game, such as volleyball, basketball, soccer, softball. Pitts uses a broad and diverse definition of "sport." According to this definition, sport is any activity, experience, or enterprise for which the primary focus is fitness, recreation, athletics, and leisure related. Activity and experience are inclusive of the many athletics, fitness, recreation, and leisure-related activities of today: car racing, horse racing, boogey-boarding, knee-boarding, water skiing, golf, walking, camping, hang gliding, throwing the boomerang, horseback riding, participating in rodeos, sailing, and many more. Enterprise is described as the management and business activities necessary for the organization and production of sport.

"Sport industry" is defined as the market in which the products offered to its buyers are fitness, sport, recreation, and leisure related. These products include goods, services, people, places, and ideas. Sport industry products include, but are not necessarily limited to, the following: fitness activity and all fitness-related goods and services; sports activity and all sports-related goods and services; recreation and leisure activity and all recre-

ation- and leisure-related goods and services; and all related management, financial, marketing, and other administration and business goods and services (Pitts, 1988; Pitts, Fielding, & Miller, 1991).

The application of all four variables of the Porter model to the massive sport industry would require quite possibly years of research and analysis. The result could be book length. For this reason, we chose to limit segmentation of the sport industry to two of Porter's variables--product segments and buyer segments. We strongly suggest that further research be conducted utilizing the complete industry segmentation model for a complete sport industry segmentation.

Definitions, descriptions, and functions of the multitude of products offered in the sport industry were collected for analysis (see, for example, the works of Comte & Stogel, 1990; DeSensi et al., 1990; and Stotlar, 1989). From their works, product functions and benefits were identified and grouped homogeneously within groups as well as heterogeneously between groups to form specific product segments. Definitions for the product segments were developed. In addition, sport products within each segment were identified and categorized.

It has been suggested by Mullin (1985) that there are

only two types of buyers of sport products: spectators and participants. Mullin's categories of sport consumers are based on selling "sports" for participation or for spectating and do not include an analysis of the complete sport industry. The findings of our study show that there are more than two categories of sport product consumers. Types of buyers in the sport industry are dependent on product segment, product variety, and product function and benefit.

RESULTS

Three segments were identified in the sport industry, and we have labeled them the Sport Performance Segment, the Sport Production Segment, and the Sport Promotion Segment. Industrial and consumer goods buyer types were identified. Figure 2 illustrates the segments identified in the sport industry.

Sport Performance Segment

As a product, "sport performance" is offered to buyers primarily in two ways: as a product for participants and as a product for spectators. These may be treated as separate industry segments due primarily to the nature of marketing participation and spectatorial products. We have placed them in one industry segment because of similarities in product function and benefit.

As a participation product, sport performance is offered to the buyer in a multitude of product offerings. The consumer may choose to participate in any number of sports or leisure activities, settings, performance (skill) levels, and market segment offerings (demographics segmentation such as an over-30 age group soccer league). Some of the settings are sports leagues, tournaments, one-day events, camps, and education classes. In the development of a list of product varieties, it is important to note that a matrix may be developed for every product variety. Figure 3 demonstrates a segmentation matrix using basketball as a product variant of sport participation and demographics as buyer type variants. With this illustration you can see that developing a complete list of product varieties in this product segment would be highly complex and require much time and paper.

In some industries, as in the sport industry, there are so many products offered that consolidation is necessary to make the list more workable. Although it is true that sports, recreation, and fitness activities can be different in definition and actual activity, almost all provide the buyer with similar functions and benefits: a workout, stress management, fun, competition, activity, or entertainment. We have focused the sport performance segment on formats through which the product may be offered. For example, basketball, volleyball, and martial arts are different activities, yet they may be offered to the buyer in similar formats, such as leagues, tournaments, or one-day events. Within each format, the product may be differentiated as it is structured to attract a particular buyer type.

As a product for spectators, sport performance is offered to consumers in four ways: spectating through personal attendance at a sport event, spectating the event via television, spectating sport event videos, and spectating a sport event indirectly through the images created in the listener's mind by the sense of hearing through radio. Spectating the event in person is considered the purest form of spectating if one considers the standard dictionary's definition of spectating. However, in sport marketing, all forms of the spectatorial product are important as each is essential to the promotion of the event, profits realized, and advertising sales.

Most spectatorial products are offered at no cost to the consumer. Consider the thousands of softball leagues, volleyball leagues, youth baseball leagues, and similar sporting situations where anyone may watch and enjoy the competition. These sporting events will most likely never change. However, recently there has been an increase in the number of events offered at a cost to the consumer, for example, pay-per-view sporting events and pay-per-order cable sports programming. As the number of opportunities to watch sporting events increases, the number of events offered at a cost will also increase as sport spectating continues to enjoy market demand.

Sport spectating in person has changed dramatically over the last twenty years. There have been improvements in facility construction, technology, and design. Before these changes, sport event spectating took place in a basic sport facility designed only for enveloping the court, arena, or field. This meant that the spectator's comfort and other needs were not considered. Seating and other need-fulfilling accommodations were designed into the facility. Today, the spectator has a range of choices: One may watch from low-cost, basic seating or from an expensive "skybox," an enclosed and private climate-controlled room with accoutrements, such as a large-screen TV, a supplied bar, food, newspapers, magazines, phones, facsimile machines, computers, plush seating, a balcony, and a private bath.

Sporting events today are offered in a variety of facilities. An "outdoor" sport, such as football, may now be viewed in an "indoor" enclosed facility. Further, if a spectator doesn't want to be distracted by the children, the sport facility management offers childcare services while the sport event is taking place. The sport facility today typically offers the consumer many accommodations and services. These have become an integral part of the sport event package.

In all sport activity, the marketer must understand that the production and consumption of the sport event or activity take place simultaneously (Mullin, 1985). This is not unique to the sport industry as it is also true of other entertainment industry products, such as live theater, dance performances, opera, and music group performances. However, these types of events require specific marketing strategies, for example, advance offering of tickets. The

		BUYER TYPES: SKILL AND AGE							
		BEGINNER				ADVANCED			
		9-12	13-18	19-25	OVER 30	9-12	13-18	19-25	OVER 30
PRODUCT: BASKETBALL TYPES:	LEAGUE								
	TOURNAMENT	YES	YES	YES	YES	YES	YES	YES	YES
	CAMP	YES	YES	NULL	NULL	YES	YES	YES	NULL
	COLLEGE	NULL	NULL	NULL	NULL	NULL	YES	YES	NULL
	PROFESSIONAL	NULL	NULL	YES	YES	NULL	YES	YES	YES

Figure 3. Sport Performance Segment: A matrix using some buyer types and product types shows possibilities

selling of tickets strictly prior to an event, and especially of a limited number of tickets, helps create demand, or the illusion of demand. The marketer must affect buyer action on three levels. At the first level, the marketer must persuade the consumer to buy the tickets needed for admission to the event. At the second level, the marketer must persuade the buyer to attend the event. One might believe that selling tickets is the only job required and assume that the buyer will attend. The marketer must not make this assumption and must work to persuade the consumer to attend. At the third level, the marketer must try to persuade the consumer to purchase other products offered before, during, and after the event. These usually are called product extensions and include items such as valet parking, souvenir merchandise, food, and beverage. The revenue from these products can be a large source of income and help offset the cost of the event.

The substitute products for attending a sport event in person are television, video, and radio. The opposite is also true: The substitute product for watching an event on television or video or listening to it on the radio is attending the event in person. In many instances, however, the owner of the sport event will regulate the ability of a local broadcasting station to televise the event. One reason, of course, is that if the event is televised and is free to the consumer, the consumer may choose not to spend the money to attend the event. Hence, television broadcasting rights contracting has developed. In this instance, a different buyer type is identified--television broadcasting companies. The event management will offer the buyer the opportunity to "buy," or televise, an event. The deals are contingent upon perceived television spectator demand. If demand is sufficient, the company will be able to "sell" advertising time; this partially pays for the cost of televising the event.

Product Segments: The following are the categories of product varieties identified in the Sport Performance Segment:

1. **Athletics:** organized sport under the auspices of organized athletics for schools and professionals that is separate from sport organized outside these two venues. Athletics includes (a) amateur sport performance as organized in the schools and colleges and (b) professional sport performance for which the performer receives a fee.

2. **Private nonsport business:** sport organized and offered by privately owned firms whose primary product is not sport. These businesses are in business for another reason and add a sport or two, such as a pub that adds a sand volleyball court and now offers leagues. There is a fine line between these firms and the ones built primarily for sports. Typically, a pub will add the sport facility if it is inexpensive and popular. When interest in the trendy sport wanes, the pub closes the sport facility and remodels it as additional pub space.

3. **Tax-supported sport organizations:** sport organized and offered by tax-supported, public organizations. Examples include city parks and recreation offices, state parks and recreation organizations, and a state Olympics organization.

4. **Membership-supported sport organizations:** sport organized and offered by membership-supported clubs or organizations. These may or may not be nonprofit organizations. Some examples are a camping club that organizes camping trips, a rugby organization that offers a rugby league, a soccer organization that offers soccer leagues, and a fencing club that offers fencing competitions.

5. **Nonprofit sport organizations:** sport offered by nonprofit firms. Examples include the International Olympic Committee, which offers the modern Olympics every four years; the Federation of Gay Games, which offers the Gay Games every four years; the Amateur Softball Association, which offers structured softball leagues and tournaments every year; the Special Olympics; the United States Soccer Association, which offers structured soccer leagues and tournaments; the YWCA and the YMCA, which offer a number of fitness and sport activities.

6. **Sport education:** Sport taught to the consumer. Some products are private lessons, clinics, sport camps, fitness camps, coaching clinics, seminars, conferences,

and sport institutes.

7. **Fitness and sport firms:** Fitness, health, wellness, and sport firms that offer participation in sports and fitness in either a single-sport or multisport setting. This includes the privately owned fitness and sports businesses. Examples are fitness centers, tennis clubs, indoor soccer centers, indoor volleyball centers, golf clubs, and resorts.

The product types identified are those products offered to the consumer as sport performance as either a participant product or a spectator product. If the sport marketer understands the benefits and functions of the product, successful sport-marketing strategies will result.

Buyer Segments: Buyer types were identified in this industry segment in both participant and spectatorial product types. Buyer types include both industrial/commercial and consumer goods categories. Some industrial and commercial buyer types identified include the following: companies that contract for fitness/wellness programs for their employees; companies that purchase large numbers of sport event tickets; companies that buy the right to broadcast sporting events; and companies that buy materials to produce sporting goods for sale to retailers or another channel.

Consumer goods buyers identified in this segment include a wide variety of buyers categorized by demographics, psychographics, life-style, language, and other factors. Buyer types of sport as a participant product may be identified using demographics. Basketball may be offered in age-group leagues, such as youth, 16 and under, 18 and under, 19 to 24, 25 to 29, over-30, over-40, and so on. Further, within each age group, more buyer types may be identified, such as female, male, and coed. Figure 3 presents an example of some buyer types of basketball available to the sport marketer using two demographics, skill level and age.

It is also interesting to note that many identifiable populations are organizing and managing their own sports leagues, events, olympics, classes, clinics, and more. Some of them are women, African Americans, Native Americans, the Jewish population, the lesbian and gay populations, and the disabled. Each population is a buyer type. The sport marketer could develop and offer products targeting each buyer type. Further, the marketer could identify even more buyer types by using demographics or psychographics, much like those used as an example in Figure 3.

Buyer types identified in sport performance offered as a spectatorial product consist of those consumers considered spectators. As was identified in sport performance offered as a participant product, the sport marketer may use demographics and psychographics to identify and segment buyer types within each of the four forms of sport event spectating available. For example, spectating the Super Bowl is offered to the following buyer types: corporate buyers with unlimited funds; corporate buyers

with limited funds; individual buyers with unlimited funds; and individual buyers with limited funds. Further, within each type, the sport marketer may identify specific buyer types by using demographics and psychographics.

If the sport marketer is successful at identifying all the buyer types that exist for a product, the marketer will succeed in formulating marketing strategies. If the sport marketer can identify potential buyer types, products may be developed to meet the needs of those types.

Sport Production Segment

Definition: This segment comprises those products necessary or desired to produce sport or to influence the level of sport or fitness performance. Some sports cannot be performed at all without certain products. Some sports could not be performed at desired levels without specific products. This creates a demand for a variety of products needed or desired for the production of sport and for influencing the level or quality of sport performance.

For example, in the production of a softball game, a participant needs some specific softball equipment—a glove, a bat, a softball. To participate in an officially organized competition, one will also need a softball facility and umpires. In addition, if participants want to improve or enhance their level of performance, they could purchase specific equipment in the belief that performance will be enhanced. Many products and prices are offered to the consumer. Softball bats are offered in a variety of materials, colors, lengths, weights, and prices. Each is offered to benefit different buyer types and consumer wants and needs. In addition, the softball player may indulge in softball-lover paraphernalia, such as softball keychains, t-shirts, bags, caps, socks, and gloves.

Another example to illustrate this is tennis and Martina Navratilova. It is questionable if Navratilova would be the all-time great champion in women's tennis if she had to use the first type of tennis racket produced, had no personal fitness trainer or weight training equipment, and was confined to playing matches in clothing that almost completely covered her. Although Navratilova is one of the greatest athletes in sports today, her success has been enhanced by high-tech equipment, training methods, and performance-enhancing apparel.

Product Segments: The following are the categories of product varieties identified in this industry segment:

1. **Outfitting products:** the equipment and apparel either required or preferred in the performance/production of sport.

   A. Equipment: Required and/or preferred, sport equipment may be inexpensive and fundamental or highly specialized, customized, and expensive.

   B. Apparel: Sports clothing and sport shoes required or referred. Again, these products may be basic and inexpensive or specialized, customized, and costly.

2. **Performance production products:** performance production products, other than outfitting products, needed or

desired for the production of sport. Sport may be produced at one of many points along a continuum. This continuum ranges from the highly sophisticated, elite performance in an expensive, high-tech facility to the weekend athlete's performance in a local homespun facility, such as a back yard. This includes the following:

A. **Fitness trainer:** The fitness trainer, whose actual title may be "trainer" or "strength and conditioning coach" or other, designs and coordinates the athlete's fitness, conditioning, and sport training program.

B. **Medical care:** The sport medicine team specializes in the care and rehabilitation of the injured athlete, regardless of level of athleticism. The sports medicine team often works with the fitness trainer in the coordination of the many facets of the athlete's life that affect the level and frequency of performance. This form of medical care used to be offered only to professional, collegiate, and high school athletes. Recently, freestanding sports medicine clinics open to the public have increased primarily due to the demand of the weekend athlete for appropriate and specialized medical care.

C. **Sport facilities:** Research has shown the negative and positive effects of the sport facility on athletic performance. Marketers will also attest to the selling performance of sports facilities. Whether for performance or for the spectator's convenience, the sport facility's condition, materials, and other factors are important in the production of sport performance. These include the sport field, court, track, pool, arena, stadium, and other facilities needed, such as concession areas, parking areas, locker rooms/dressing rooms, media provisions, officials needs, and private boxes or rooms.

D. **Governing bodies and officials:** The growth of sport has demanded a parallel growth of the structure and limits within which the sport may be performed. Governance of sport influences fair play and decreases risk of injury. The organization or sport, regardless of the size of the production or the level of performance, requires rules, regulations, policies, and compliance personnel. The governing body provides the guidelines for the structure and format of the sport and defines all aspects of the sport, such as performance rules, facility requirements, equipment regulation, reward and compensation guidelines, and even performance standards in some cases.

Many rules of sports and sport equipment are modified today to increase the marketability of the sport. Some examples include the Special Olympics, in which almost all rules of sports and equipment have been modified; men's basketball, in which the height of the basket has remained 10 feet to encourage crowd-pleasing dunks; women's basketball, in which the ball is smaller than the men's basketball in order to enhance crowd-pleasing skills; and marathons that include or hold a separate marathon for wheelchair athletes.

Buyer segments: Buyer types include those consumers who need or want outfitting or performance production products. Buyer types identified include both consumer goods buyers and commercial and industrial buyers. Two consumer goods buyer types identified include (a) sport participants of all demographically and psychographically identified segments and (b) gift shoppers--those consumers looking to purchase these kinds of products as gifts for birthday, Christmas, or other occasion. Some commercial and industrial buyers include high school and college athletic departments, professional sport firms, tax-supported sport organizations, membership-supported sport organizations, nonprofit sport organizations, sport educators, fitness and sport firms, private nonsport firms offering sport as a secondary product, and private nonsport firms.

Sport Promotion Segment

Definition: This segment comprises those products used in the promotion of sport industry products. Sport or fitness activity can exist without promotion. However, it is enhanced, promoted, and in some cases partially funded by promotion products. Sales of sport- and fitness-related goods and services are certainly affected by promotion. The competitors in all segments of the sport industry use a variety of promotion products and tactics. This need to compete creates a demand for promotional products, means, methods, and people who specialize in promotion, marketing, public relations, and other related areas.

Product Segments: The following are the categories of product varieties identified in this industry segment;

1. **Promotional merchandising products:** Promotional merchandise is strategically created to promote sport or a sport product. For example, sport managers or marketers use a variety of promotional merchandise products to promote and market sporting events, organizations, and even individual sport celebrities. Included might be t-shirts, cups, key rings, caps, jackets, blankets, and an event program (a printed program). Other examples include lamps, bumper stickers, sweats, decals, and even shoes. Typically, the merchandise is printed with the logo or other identifying mark of the sport organization or product.

2. **Promotional events:** Planned event or events to coincide with or to bring attention to a sporting event or to a sport product. Examples include holding a concert by a popular star or group in conjunction with a sport event; having a sport star appearance in conjunction with a sport event; having a well-known coach or athlete attend the opening of a sport facility; "give-aways," as they are called in sport marketing, wherein the marketer gives away something, such as caps, to people to attend a sporting event or a sport facility; promoting "tailgating" (partying using the tailgate of a vehicle) by offering specific areas in the parking lot and other benefits, such as free ice, to those tailgaters

who arrive during a specific time period; giving a barbecue to sport club members; and giving milestone banquets.

3. **The media:** Marketers of sport and of other sport products use the media as promotional vehicles for the sport, sporting event, or sport product. At the same time, media use sport, sport figures, sporting events, or sport products to promote their product. Sometimes, as in radio and TV, fees are paid for the right to broadcast a sporting event. This may be achieved at a cost to management of the sporting event, an exchange of goods, such as tickets, or by other means. Included here are (a) print media (i.e., newspapers, magazines, trade journals) and (b) audio/visual media (i.e., radio, TV).

4. **Sponsorship:** Full or partial funding of sport-related expenses in return for certain promotional gains. This is an exchange relationship. Sponsorship helps defray the expenses of a sporting event, a sport facility, or an athlete. Promotional gains might include advertising or other promotional means for the sponsor or an exchange of other goods or services. There are various sponsorship avenues, some of which are as follows:

   A. **Single event sponsorship:** A single event is sponsored.

   B. **Multiple event sponsorship:** Two or more events are sponsored.

   C. **Single team sponsorship:** A single team is sponsored.

   D. **Individual sponsorship:** One individual is sponsored.

   E. **Circuit or league sponsorship:** A full league or an entire circuit is sponsored.

   F. **Shared sponsorship:** Two or more sponsors sponsor an event, team, individual, league, or circuit. This has become popular because the total cost of an event is shared and is therefore less expensive for each sponsor.

5. **Endorsement:** A fee is paid, or goods and/or services are traded for the use of an individual or other to endorse—show support for—a product. The product may or may not be a sport product. Use of the endorser brings attention to the product by capitalizing on the popularity of the endorser. Some examples are the use of Chris Evert to promote tennis rackets, the use of Michael Jordan to promote Nike shoes, and the use of Chuck Yeager to promote motor oil. There are different categories of endorsement. Those categories identified are:

   A. **Individual endorsement:** Use of an athlete, coach, owner, or other individual person.

   B. **Team endorsement:** Use of a full team.

   C. **Full organization:** Use of an entire organization, such as the NCAA, the NFL, the IOC, or USOC.

   D. **Nonspecific-sport use:** The use of any sport, without the use of well-known figures or teams or organizations, to promote a product.

Buyer Segments: Buyer types include both commercial/industrial and consumer goods buyers. The commercial/industrial buyers include those sport businesses that use promotional methods to promote their products. Some examples are high school athletic departments, college athletic departments, professional sports organizations, private sport businesses, and tax-supported sport organizations. Consumer goods buyers include those who purchase promotional merchandise for individual use. Some examples include gift buyers, those who purchase merchandise as a gift; collector buyers, those who purchase promotional merchandise as a collector item; and "fan" buyers, those who identify themselves as "fans" of a particular team or sport.

SUMMARY and RECOMMENDATIONS

The purpose of this investigation was to apply Porter's industry segmentation theory to the sport industry and to develop an initial sport industry segment model. The model developed in this study, using only a portion of Porter's theory, represents a new perspective of the industry and should be viewed as an initial framework for further investigation.

Although it seems easy to accept traditional definitions and categorization of products and consumers in the sport industry, this acceptance is perhaps the most important catalyst for analyzing the industry from different perspectives. As an example, the addition of an over-30 women's category in a soccer league reflects the identification of a new buyer type. The analysis should show that many female soccer players do not want to stop playing soccer just because they turn 30. Their desire for type of competitor has most likely changed; that is, they may now choose to compete against a similar age group instead of competing against the 20-year-olds. In this example, the use of just one demographic creates a new buyer type and should point to a few more: men's over-30 and coed over-30. This can be taken a step further. Are there 40-year-olds who play soccer? If not today, what about when the 30-year-olds begin to turn 40?

The identification of a new buyer type does not mean, however, that the firm must develop a product for that type. It does mean that the sport marketer knows that the buyer type exists and may begin considering the feasibility of adding a product to meet buyer want.

Challenges to the sport marketer in using segmentation theory are to identify new ways of segmenting the industry and to find new ways of combining segments. This could lead to the discovery of a variety of segments and, perhaps, of more meaningful segments. For example, this may include discovering a new use for an existing product, a new buyer type for an existing product, or a buyer type but no existing product. This kind of analysis will ascertain the future possibilities for the company.

Although we were able to use a portion of Porter's (1985) theory to identify product segments and buyer segments in the sport industry, we recommend an analysis of the sport industry using all of Porter's model. We also recommend investigation of the sport industry using other industry segmentation models. Investigations should build upon the research presented here. Scholarly analysis could result in different and perhaps more complete analysis of the sport industry. The very purpose of industry segmentation is that it is to be used as "an analytical tool, not an end in itself" (Porter, 1985, p.254).

REFERENCES

Comte, E., & Stogel, C. (1990, January 1). Sports: A $63.1 billion industry. *The Sporting News*, pp. 60-61.

Day, G.S., Shocker, A.D., & Srivastava, R.K. (1979). Customer-oriented approaches to identifying product-markets. *Journal of Marketing, 43* (4), 8-19.

DeSensi, J.T., Kelley, D.R., Blanton, M.D., & Beitel, P.A. (1990). Sport management curricular evaluation and needs assessment: A multifaceted approach. *Journal of Sport Management, 4*(1), 31-58.

Fielding, L.W., Pitts, B.G., & Miller, L.K. (1991, February-March). *Learning about market penetration and market development from successful companies: Hillerich and Bradsby from Buster Brown Bat to the Babe Ruth autograph model 1907-1923.* Paper presented at the International Conference for Sport Business, Columbia, SC.

McCarthy, E.J., & Perrault, W.D. (1990). *Basic marketing.* Homewood, IL: Irwin Publishers.

Mullin, B. (1985). Characteristics of sport marketing. In G. Lewis, & H. Appenzeller, (Eds.), *Successful sport management.* Charlottesville, VA: The Michie Company.

Parks, J.B., & Zanger, B.R.K. (Eds.). (1990). *Sport & fitness management: Career strategies and professional content.* Champaign, IL: Human Kinetics Publishers, Inc.

Pitts, B.G. (1988). *Sport product markets.* Unpublished manuscript, University of Louisville.

Pitts, B. G., Fielding, L. W., & Miller, L.K. (1991, June). *Sport product-markets: A conceptual model.* Paper presented at the conference of the North American Society for Sport Management, Ottawa, Canada.

Porter, M.E. (1985). *Competitive advantage: Creating and sustaining superior performance.* New York: The Free Press.

Stotlar, D.K. (1989). *Successful sport marketing and sponsorship plans.* Dubuque, IA: Wm. C. Brown Publishers.